Christian History

A Captivating Guide to the History of Christianity, Kings of Israel and Judah, and Queen of Sheba

Free Bonus from Captivating History (Available for a Limited time)

Hi History Lovers!

Now you have a chance to join our exclusive history list so you can get your first history ebook for free as well as discounts and a potential to get more history books for free! Simply visit the link below to join.

Captivatinghistory.com/ebook

Also, make sure to follow us on Facebook, Twitter and Youtube by searching for Captivating History.

Contents

Part 1: History of Christianity

A Captivating Guide to Crucial Moments in Christian History, Including Events Such as the Life and Teachings of Jesus Christ, the Early Church, and the Reformation

Introduction

Who would have thought that from its humble beginnings as a small group of followers of a Jewish man called Jesus that Christianity would become, less than two thousand years later, the most widespread religion on Earth?

Around thirty-one percent of the world's population is Christian today, which would equate to more than two billion people, encompassing practically all of the countries in every continent. Each year, on December 25, according to our modern calendar, Christians all over the world celebrate a very special event: Jesus' birthday. This date—Christmas—marks the beginning of it all, the starting point of an epic journey that has radically changed history. However, perhaps this was not where it actually started; others might say that his story began way before, that he was the much-anticipated Messiah for many centuries before his birth, which Judaic scriptures had predicted since ancient times. One way or the other, the course of human development has definitely been altered since a couple of millennia ago. Even in those places where this religion was not a dominant feature at some point in their history or never has been, like the Americas at the time of Christopher Columbus or Eastern Asia, Christianity exerted an influence that altered their traditional ways of life.

From its origins in the eastern realms of the Roman Empire and then its expansion into Europe on one side of the world and all the way to India and China on the other, Christianity has never stopped taking in new believers in its two-thousand-year history.

What is Christianity's appeal? Why would it become this popular and entrenched in so many human minds and spirits?

For one, Christianity "proclaims itself as intended for all men without distinction of race or caste."[i] And for believers, as well as for those who do not have faith in Jesus as God's son or even for those who do not follow any religious creed, the fact is that this man's life—who can also be seen by some as God's son and God himself—is fascinating. He managed to motivate a strong group of firm followers into spreading his words, teachings, and deeds in such a way that it still appeals to billions around the world today.

Christianity's birth and development is a vast, complex story filled with setbacks and contradictions but also with triumphs. It is intricately entwined with the world's development over the last two thousand years, encompassing entire societies, helping to build and destroy empires, and molding the spiritual lives of people of all races and cultures. The following chapters will reveal the main aspects surrounding this fascinating saga.

Chapter 1 –Prophecies with an Announced birth

Ancient Predictions of a Special King

For centuries before Jesus Christ's birth, some two thousand years ago, people of the Jewish faith had been expecting what they called the Messiah—a man or even God himself coming down to Earth in order to save humankind. The source for these messianic prophecies is contained in the Hebrew Bible, the Tanakh or Mikra, which consists of three parts summing up twenty-four books: the Torah, also known as the Book of Moses; the Nevi'im, where the prophets' revelations were laid down; and the Ketuvim, containing Psalms, Ecclesiastes and other writings.

The word Tanakh is actually an acronym, formed with the first letter of the three subdivisions of the authoritative Hebrew and Aramaic Masoretic Texts it contains: T for Torah, N for Nevi'im, and K for Ketuvim.[ii] These documents were first written down around 200 BCE. Before that, though, they had been passed on from one generation to the other in verbal form.

This sacred manuscript is basically the content of what Christians know as the Old Testament, the first part of the Christian Bible. Its division into chapters and versicles came later on.

At some point, the Tanakh also contained the deuterocanonical books, which comprise texts such as the Books of the Maccabees, the Book of Ezra, the Book of Ecclesiasticus, and Psalm 151, among others. Deuterocanonical literally means "second-degree canonical" from the Greek words of Sumerian origin *deutero*, defined as "secondary," and *canon*, which can be translated as "rule" or "measuring stick." Even though these added texts to the original Torah were accepted as dogma back then, they had lesser importance.

The deuterocanonical books were first included in the Septuagint, the Greek translation of the Torah, which was written in the third century BCE during the Hellenistic period. Around the year 95 CE, chief Jewish rabbis supposedly gathered in the Council of Jamnia (this meeting has not been historically confirmed) had already decided to exclude them as part of their sacred texts, alleging that they had been written in Greek and not in the original Jewish language.

Most Protestant churches do not accept the deuterocanonical books either, believing them to be apocryphal and mainly unverified accounts that do not belong within the canonical or dogmatically approved Masoretic Text of the ancient Tanakh. However, the Catholic Church, the Anglicans, the Eastern Orthodox Church, and the Assyrian Church of the East, among others, do accept them and consider them to be canonical.

The second part of the Christian Bible, the New Testament, contains—among several other scriptures—four different accounts on Jesus' life and teachings. These are known as the Gospels, written by Luke, Matthew, Mark, and John. The stories of the first three are relatively similar, so they are regarded as the synoptic Gospels because a synopsis, or summary, could be made with all of them put together. Many of their passages resemble each other, with some even having the exact same writing. On the other hand, the Gospel of John varies significantly from the first three in many of its stories.

The collection of predictions pointed out by prophets such as Samuel, Jeremiah, Daniel, and Isaiah contained in the Old Testament are sanctioned by all Christians nowadays. These men foretold that a Messiah would restore the kingdom of God on Earth and that from then on, this kingdom would "last forever." They also believed this savior would come from the House of David, the famed Jewish king who lived around 1000 BCE in what many call "the Golden Age of Israel." The Old Testament states that Prophet Nathan told David that "the Lord Himself will establish a house for you…I will raise up your offspring to succeed you…I will establish his kingdom. He is the one who will build a house for my Name, and I will establish the throne of his kingdom forever" (2 Samuel 7).

Both the lineage of Mary and Joseph, Jesus' mother and earthly father, can be traced back to King David himself. In the New Testament, only Matthew and Luke provide this genealogy, and even then, they differ somewhat, which has made some modern scholars discard this David-to-Jesus lineage as an invention. Much has certainly been discussed regarding this point, yet the House of David extracts noted down in the Bible has made this an intrinsic part of Christianity's doctrine and dogma and of its axiomatic teachings.

Eighth-century BCE prophet Isaiah is especially considered to have predicted the coming of Christ. The Old Testament cites him as saying that "For to us a child is born, to us a son is given; and the government shall be upon his shoulder, and his name shall be called Wonderful Counselor, Mighty God, Everlasting Father, Prince of Peace. Of the increase of his government and of peace there will be no end, on the throne of David and over his kingdom, to establish it and to uphold it with justice and with righteousness from this time forth and forevermore" (Isaiah 9:6-7). This extract is supremely important for Christians because it clearly states some of the most important issues surrounding Jesus as the son of God and his eternal kingdom. This Isaiah verse is inevitably cited during every Christmas celebration. The passage clearly talks about incarnation and the divinity of Christ, who could rule a kingdom forever. None of the earthly Jewish kings actually fit the prophecies, but Jesus' life and ideas did align with this messianic image in quite a perfect way.

As to who would be this Messiah is key to understanding when Judaism and Christianity started going their own ways. Those who believe in the teachings of Judaism are still waiting for that savior to arrive. The idea of this savior for the Jewish people is to reestablish a "united kingdom" with all of the dispersed twelve Hebrew tribes of antiquity, yet they believe the one to do so should be a human being of flesh and blood, an earthly physical king. The followers of Jesus Christ decided otherwise. How would their kingdom be? Yes, it would be eternal, but it would be for all the people on Earth, not only the Jewish people, and it would not be dominated by a human being but by God himself. He would be the ultimate king, the one Isaiah talked about, the one who would rule over everyone willing to follow him, and these followers did not need to be people of Hebrew descent exclusively.

So, Jesus Christ was born a Jew and within the Jewish religion and traditions. The circumstances surrounding his birth was also prophesied. For example, some ancient prophets had already described that this savior of humanity would come from a "virgin conception." Isaiah told Ahaziah, Israel's king during his time, that "therefore the Lord himself shall give you a sign; behold, a virgin shall conceive, and bear a son, and shall call his name Immanuel" (Isaiah 7:13). Immanuel means "God with us."

A Virgin Is with Child

The events surrounding the birth of Jesus are perhaps some of the most well-known accounts of all times. Part of its appeal comes from the fact that it borrows many concepts from other religions and creeds, such as the miraculous birth of a god or "chosen one," for example—a notion that can also be seen in Zoroastrian, Egyptian, Hindu, and Buddhist beliefs.

Jesus' mother, Mary, was a young Jewish woman from the Galilean town of Nazareth which was located in the northern part of modern-day Israel, an area which in the first century BCE was part of the Roman Empire. It is in this place where an angel, Gabriel, announced to Mary that she would conceive and give birth to a child and that he would be the son of God. She told Gabriel this could not be since she was a virgin, and he answered that the conception would be possible because "the Holy Spirit will come on you" (Luke 1:35). Gabriel instructed her that this son was to be called "the Son of the Most High." Mary ended up naming him Jesus, "Yeshua" in Aramaic, a contraction of *Yehoshuah*, which means "Yhwh is salvation." This was a common name in Judea back then.

Mary was betrothed at that moment to Joseph, also a Jewish man whose lineage was linked to King David. There is not much information about him available, however. Joseph is barely mentioned in the Gospels of Luke and Matthew, and there are no references to him in the other two. He is believed to have been born somewhere around 100 BCE and that he was a carpenter or wood craftsman.

Apart from the prophecies stated in the Old Testament, only two of the Gospels—again, Luke and Matthew—talk about Mary's miraculous conception. However, both accounts are quite different.

Matthew focuses more on Joseph, mentioning how he had found out that Mary was pregnant just when they were about to get married. He states that at first Joseph decided to break the engagement discreetly so as not to shame her in public. During those times, if word got out that a woman had a child out of wedlock, she would be stoned to death. Matthew then relates that an angel visited Joseph and told him not to worry, that the child Mary carried was the son of God, conceived by the Holy Spirit, so Joseph decided to stay with her and become that child's earthly father. Matthew also writes that he did not have "marital relations with her before she gave birth," loosely implying they did become a couple after that.

On the other hand, the Gospel of Luke is the only stating the entire dialogue between Mary and the angel Gabriel, where she explicitly says that she is a virgin. With regard to Joseph, Luke simply mentions that Mary was "promised in marriage" to him, not mentioning anything about Joseph's own conversation with the angel.

There are three important concepts—Immaculate Conception, virginal conception, and virgin birth— that relate to Mary's own birth, her pregnancy, and the moment when she goes into labor.

Matthew states that Mary became pregnant through the Holy Spirit and not by having sexual intercourse with Joseph, this being the so-called virginal conception. "While his mother Mary was engaged to Joseph, but before they came together, she was found to be pregnant through the Holy Spirit" (Matt. 1:18-20).

The "virgin birth" refers to the fact that Mary was a virgin when she conceived Jesus and that she also remained a virgin until after the birth of her child. Catholic Church doctrine claims that she stayed celibate throughout her whole life, meaning she did not have intercourse with Joseph at any time—thus the Catholic Church's description of Mary being the "ever-virgin" (*Aeiparthenos* in Greek, a term widely used in Orthodox liturgy, although not all Orthodox churches accept the term nowadays).

These concepts are very deeply intertwined with the Catholic Immaculate Conception doctrine, which means that Mary was not only a virgin but also free from original sin. The Old Testament asserts that all human beings since Adam and Eve have been living in sin. Yet Mary, Jesus, and his cousin, John the Baptist, were exempt from it. This doctrine was incorporated into the Roman Catholic creed in 1854 under Pope Pius IX's rule. He set the dogma that "the most Blessed Virgin Mary was, from the first moment of her conception, by a singular grace and privilege of almighty God and by virtue of the merits of Jesus Christ, Savior of the human race, preserved immune from all stain of original sin."[iii]

All Christians basically agree on the virginal conception doctrine, yet the concepts of Mary's Immaculate Conception and virgin birth are not accepted by most Protestant churches. All of these ideas have also been widely discussed and analyzed by theologians, historians, and academics. They have been at the core of many debates, particularly during the first three centuries after the death of Christ, but it still continues to this day.

There was another announcement the angel Gabriel told Mary at the time of his visit: that her cousin, Elizabeth, was also going to give birth to a child even though she was already of advanced age. So, Mary went to visit her. The moment Elizabeth set eyes on her cousin, she unequivocally knew that Mary was pregnant as well and that she was with the child of God. "You are the most blessed of all women, and blessed is the child that you will have. I feel blessed that the mother of my Lord is visiting me. As soon as I heard your greeting, I felt the baby jump for joy," she stated (Luke 1:42-45).

The angel Gabriel had appeared to Elizabeth's husband, Zechariah, beforehand, telling him that she would bear a child. He instructed that the baby was to be named John and informed Zechariah that his birth would be without original sin (that the baby would be filled with the Holy Spirit). "He will be your pride and joy, and many people will be glad that he was born. As far as the Lord is concerned, he will be a great man...He will be filled with the Holy Spirit even before he is born. He will bring many people in Israel back to the Lord their God...he will prepare the people for their Lord," he told Zechariah (Luke 1:13-17).

This baby, in fact, eventually played an important role in Jesus' life. He went on to become John the Baptist, who baptized his distant cousin many years later in the Jordan River, and this is probably why he received the special gift of being born without original sin. According to the Gospels, when Jesus came out of the water, John "saw heaven split open and the Spirit coming down to him as a dove" (Mark 1:10).

The Christian Church grasped this important symbolism later on in order to develop the concept of the Trinity, which states that although God is one, it is represented in three consubstantial entities: The Father, the Son (Jesus Christ), and the Holy Spirit. Hence, people are baptized with the renowned Trinitarian formula "in the name of the Father, and of the Son, and of the Holy Spirit."

The Child Is Born

The events surrounding Jesus' birth were quite dramatic and profoundly beautiful as well. A short while before Mary was due, Roman Emperor Augustus sent out a decree stating that a census was to be made within the Roman provinces. Since Joseph's family was from Bethlehem, he had to go back there in order to comply with the emperor's instructions. It was a very long and arduous trip from Nazareth, made especially difficult with a heavily pregnant wife. Once they arrived, all of the inns were completely full. There was nowhere to stay, and no one seemed to care that this very young woman, who had just arrived from an exhausting journey, was about to give birth (estimates indicate that Mary was between fourteen and sixteen at the time).

The only shelter Joseph managed to procure was a stable, and there—among a donkey, an ox, and sheep—Mary delivered Jesus Christ. She "wrapped him in bands of cloth, and laid him in a manger" (Luke 2:6-7). Soon afterward, a group of shepherds arrived. They said an angel had told them that they needed to see "the Messiah, the Lord" (Luke 1:11).

Sometime after Jesus' birth, the group received another very special visit: three Wise Men—Magi or Kings as they are also known—arrived from faraway stretches of the world, wanting to see the son of God and bearing lavish gifts. Their names were not mentioned in the Gospels, but later accounts state them as being Melchior from Persia, Gaspar from India, and Balthazar from Arabia. Depending on the Church, they receive other names as well. For example, Syrian Christians refer to them as Larvandad, Gushnasaph, and Hormisdas. Other Eastern churches call them Hor, Karsudan, and Basanater, and the Armenian Catholics use the names Kagpha, Badadakharida, and Badadilma.

Who were these exotic men, though? What is their significance? Luke, the most accurate narrator of Jesus' life, never mentioned them, so the information we have about Melchior, Gaspar, and Balthazar are from vague accounts stated in Matthew's Gospel. There are elements in their story which were most surely borrowed from other traditions. A Persian belief, involving a magus (the singular form of magi; this is also what members of a priestly caste in ancient Persia were called), states that the sighting of a star predicted the birth of a ruler, and some Central Asian communities also claimed they were descendants of a magus. There were also many kings who had astrologers—many times called magi—in their courts, all interpreting the elements from heaven in their own ways.

In sum, there is little historical information on these three men, but their admittedly romantic story is quite appealing and has cast a widespread spell throughout the centuries. Their epic journey, the way they were guided from remote areas toward this baby called Jesus, and their rich clothing and lavish gifts have long fascinated and roused the imagination of many over the centuries.

According to the Gospel of Matthew, the Magi arrived from the east into Jerusalem and asked, "Where is the one who was born to be the king of the Jews? We saw his star rising and have come to worship him" (Matt. 2:1-12).

The ruler of the Judean province at the time, King Herod I, heard about these men, and anxious to know where this boy had been born, he summoned the Magi. They told him this place was Bethlehem, and King Herod asked them to come back to him after finding out the exact location of the boy because he "may go and worship him too." That was not his intention at all, though; what he really wanted was to kill this so-called Messiah as Herod was afraid he might grow up and grab his throne. However, the Wise Men received a warning from God regarding Herod, telling them not to go back to him. So, after visiting Jesus, they left Judea down another road so as not to encounter this king again.

In order for the Wise Men to find the baby Jesus, Matthew mentions the rise of a bright star at the time of the Messiah's birth. This radiant light, now known as the Star of Bethlehem or the Christmas Star, was also prophesied in the Old Testament. The Book of Numbers, for example, states that "A Star shall come out of Jacob; a Scepter shall rise out of Israel."

Matthew describes that this star the Magi had been seeing led them to Jesus, and when they entered the stable, they "bowed down and worshipped him. Then they opened their treasure chests and offered him gifts of gold, frankincense, and myrrh." This passage of Jesus' birth is a beautiful and elaborate one, although it was a bit of a materialistic way to honor him as the king among kings—he received gifts way beyond anything he or his parents could ever expect to possess during their entire lives.

The elements around Jesus' birth—the stable, animals, shepherds, the Wise Men, the omnipresent angel Gabriel, and the star—all form the immensely famous scene of the Nativity as it is called by Christians after Pope Sixtus III had one built in Rome back in 432 CE. This is one of the most depicted settings in the entire world, and it has been captured by thousands of artists in all kinds of works of art—paintings, sculptures, stained glass, and mosaics—as well as staged by children and adults during Christmastime at churches, schools, and theaters.

The Wise Men are so famous that they have a separate celebration twelve days after December 25 —that is, on January 6, and in the Eastern Orthodox Churches on January 12. It is logical to state that they did not arrive on the exact day as Jesus' birth but some time afterward. A few accounts assert that this visit may have even been a couple of years later.

This special celebration, called Epiphany or Kings' Day, is commemorated in many different ways around the globe. Spanish and Latin American children receive candy and other gifts, and Italy awaits a good witch, *La Befana*, who also brings gifts. Ethiopians celebrate *Timkat* a couple of weeks later, following the tradition that the Wise Men brought the Ark of the Covenant, a gold-covered wooden chest that contains the stone tablets of the Ten Commandments, to their country. In some Eastern Orthodox countries, young men dive into cold waters to go after crosses that have been thrown in.

So, Jesus' birth has been a cause for numerous festivities, traditions, and much gift-giving that is still celebrated today. These series of holidays over a period of more than one month aim to cherish what Christians see as God himself coming down to Earth in order to save the world.

Many theories and investigations have tried to pinpoint the exact year of Jesus' birth. Although officially set at 1 CE, New Testament scholars have come to the general consensus that, at least from a historical point of view, this is not the real date. His birth was most likely between 6 and 4 BCE, basically due to the historical fact that King Herod died in 4 BCE.

Scholars and astronomers have also studied the presence of different astronomical events during those centuries to try and establish which could have been the Star of Bethlehem. Some argue that it may have coincided with the passing of a comet or that it could have been several other stellar objects in the years around Jesus' birth.

For example, astronomer Colin Humphreys proposed that the fabled star was actually a bright, slow-moving comet appearing in the constellation of Capricorn, which Chinese observers recorded in 5 BCE. Other hypotheses state that in 4 BCE a supernova occurring in the Andromeda Galaxy became visible, as well as several conjunctions of stars and planets. There are historical records showing that during that century Chinese and Korean astronomers observed a nova (a young star which is normally very bright) from the constellation of Aquila.

Astronomer Michael Molnar proposed the year 6 BCE as the likely year of Jesus' birth by using these key astronomical indicators as well as astrological and historical ones. University of Sheffield astronomer David Hughes, who has been studying this phenomenon since the 1970s, concludes that it was the conjunction of several occurrences called a triple conjunction. In this instance, it was when the planets Jupiter and Saturn aligned themselves with the Sun and the Earth three times throughout a short period of time, and it probably happened in 5 BCE. This incident normally occurs once every nine hundred years, so it would have held quite the impact on those that saw it.

The fact is that much has been said, interpreted, and written regarding the Star of Bethlehem, yet what actually perseveres is the great symbolic significance it has for Christians—one of heaven itself pronouncing the birth of a ruler by beaming a wondrous, shining star upon Earth.

For about the first three hundred and fifty years after Jesus was born, his birthday—the highly popular Christmas festivity—was not celebrated. The Bible never actually states the time of the year in which he was born, but historians have been able to analyze several facts in order to deduct the month of Jesus' birth. British theologian Ian Paul remarks that "the first clue comes in noting the relation between the births of Jesus and John the Baptist."[iv] After calculating the time John's father had to serve as a priest in the temple and how far apart Elizabeth and Mary were in their own pregnancies, the logical conclusion is that Jesus was probably born in September— thus, he would have been conceived in December. This aligns with other circumstances like, for example, the fact that shepherds were present when Jesus was born. They were still out in the open, something that would not have been possible in winter.

It was only in the fourth century CE—when the Romans adopted the Christian religion—that Church officials decided to start honoring the birth of Jesus. Probably out of practicality and convenience, they borrowed dates and traditions from pagan holidays, like mistletoe, gift-giving, special dining, partying, decorating houses, and lighting candles.

One of the most important Roman feasts was Saturnalia, which celebrated the winter solstice, which would have been December 25 on the Roman calendar. Adapting Jesus' birthday to this date was most assuredly a very popular move back then.

Tree lighting and decorations were also other pagan traditions that came from the northern European countries where winter was especially harsh. These communities celebrated the return of life, those first days after the winter solstice when days started growing longer, by placing candles on evergreen trees such as pines. When Christianity came about, they symbolically adapted this tree tradition to become the Biblical "tree of paradise" and began hanging red apples on them—yes, the same ones Eve tempted Adam with. Christians adapted this idea later on by placing "little red balls on green trees," as American historian Kenneth C. Davis puts it.

During the Middle Ages, Christmas celebrations already had a religious significance, although they still carried much pagan and folk flavor. As many of the festivities were still secular in spirit, the Church decided to start curbing this tendency by injecting religious meaning into many of the popular stories, legends, and customs. For example, harvest and midwinter songs were adapted to carry a Christian message. They also preached against the excessive merrymaking most people set out to have during the harsh winter season.

Puritans in the United States were so knowledgeable about Christmas' pagan origins that they actually banned the festivity for about twenty years in the seventeenth century. Yet the celebration was too popular to go against, so it was reinstated a short while after.

In the nineteenth century, Christmas celebrations became a standard celebration among Christian communities all around the world after receiving a special boost during Britain's Victorian era.

With regard to this "birthday of Jesus" controversy, Ian Paul soothes believers. "Does this all mean we are wasting our time celebrating Christmas in December? Not at all. The main point of Christmas is not *chronology* but *theology*."[v]

Chapter 2 – Life and Teachings of Jesus Christ

After the relatively extensive accounts of Mary's conception, her life while pregnant, and Jesus Christ's birth, there is no information at all in any of the Gospels regarding his childhood except for two important segments: how he managed to flee from King Herod and his famous speech at the temple. Again, only Matthew and Luke talk about this part of his life, and each one does so in their own particular way. Matthew describes the family's escape to Egypt, while Luke relates Simeon's and Anna's prophecies when they met Jesus as a young child and also describes his episode at the temple when he was twelve years old.

A Narrow Escape from Death

When King Herod found out that the Magi had decided to elude him and not tell him the exact whereabouts of that Messiah that had been born, which Herod believed would threaten his kingdom in the future, he went into a rage. Herod then ordered the unspeakable: If he could not find that one child, why not kill all the ones that could be him! Matthew relates in his Gospel that Judea's king "sent soldiers to kill all the boys two years old and younger in or near

Bethlehem. This matched the exact time he had learned from the Wise Men" (Matt 2:16).

This horrific chapter in Roman-Jewish history has not been corroborated by parallel historical accounts, so some scholars have been quick to claim this massacre was not actually true. King Herod was one of the few relevant figures of that time to have a complete biography written about him. The famous Roman-Jewish historian of the first century, Flavius Josephus (37–100 CE), wrote extensively on Herod, but he never mentioned the infamous "slaughter of the innocents."

Yet this reason alone is not enough to conclude it could not have happened, at least according to historian Paul Maier, a former professor of ancient history at Western Michigan University. Maier states that Herod was a builder of great monuments (the reconstruction of the Second Temple of Jerusalem was one of his projects, of which a segment, the famous Wailing Wall, still remains). He was an accomplished diplomat and politician as well but also had a very complicated family life. Herod took ten wives and bore many male heirs, all of which were constantly competing against each other for the throne. In this venomous scenario, there were also numerous scheming uncles, cousins, and even mothers-in-law. Herod sometimes needed to take matters in his own hands in order to preserve order within his reign. For instance, he had his favorite wife, Mariamne, her mother, and the three sons they had together all killed.

Also, later in life when Herod was already ill and about to die, Flavius Josephus does describe a "grisly" chapter that would convey his bloodthirsty and quite cruel character. Maier describes him here:

> He was paranoid, though he did have some grasp of reality. For instance, he was worried that nobody would mourn his own death. Of course, that shows how deadly accurate he was. They were preparing a general celebration. And nobody likes to die knowing that they are going to dance on…He

invites his sister Salome in and he says, "I want you to arrest all the Jewish leaders in the land and imprison them in the hippodrome just below the palace here."...And so she does so and then she says, "Brother, why am I doing this?" And Herod says, "Well, I know that when I die the Jews are going to rejoice. So I want to give them something to cry about." And so he wants these leaders all executed in that hippodrome so that there will be thousands of households weeping at the time Herod the Great dies."[vi]

It is a true historical fact that he did go on to execute all of the people who had gathered. But why would Flavius Josephus recount this horrific chapter in Herod's life but not the killing of hundreds of innocent children? Maier makes it clear that, in all cases, the massacre would have been about a dozen boys at the most, not hundreds, since Bethlehem was a very small town. With the normally high infant death rate of the time, there were certainly not many boys alive anyway. So, maybe Flavius Josephus simply did not believe this incident—among the many bloody ones Herod took part of in his life—had enough merit to be mentioned. In any case, Maier reminds us that "as we say in the profession [of historians], absence of evidence is not evidence of absence."

Historically accurate or not, the Gospel of Matthew relates that the angel Gabriel comes to the rescue once again. He appeared before Joseph and told him to "take the child and his mother, and flee to Egypt. Stay there until I tell you, because Herod intends to search for the child and kill him" (Matt. 2:13).

So, Mary, Joseph, and baby Jesus left for Egypt and stayed there until King Herod died. They then decided to go back to Israel, but— no surprise here—Joseph was still very wary of Herod's son who succeeded the throne. So, Joseph decided to avoid Jerusalem and set his way toward Nazareth, the town he had lived in when he married Mary, which was located in the region of Galilee. This isolated village, which according to recent excavations had only about fifty houses, is where Jesus spent his childhood. During this time in history, it was customary to add either the father's name or the place of origin, thus, "in his lifetime Jesus was called Jesus son of Joseph (Luke 4:22; John 1:45, 6:42), Jesus of Nazareth (Acts 10:38), or Jesus the Nazarene (Mark 1:24; Luke 24:19)."[vii]

A Special Child

It was customary for the Jewish people to frequently travel to the temple in Jerusalem, especially during festivities such as Passover.

Luke recounts three interesting episodes in Jesus' childhood, two of which are relatively little talked about. They are related to the prophecy tradition within the Jewish people.

A man named Simeon and a woman named Anna bumped into Mary and Joseph with their young boy at the temple in different periods of time. On each occasion, their respective choice of words impressed the parents because both talked of Jesus as a God and a person who would bring salvation to the people. Neither of them knew about the revelations Mary and Joseph had received at the time of Jesus' conception and birth, which—due to the normal circumstances of the time—were jealously kept a secret. These episodes are known as Simeon's and Anna's Prophecies (Luke 2:25-40).

It is also Luke who talks about the time when Jesus experienced his own *Home Alone* episode. Joseph and Mary had gone to Jerusalem with a large group of relatives for the Passover festival. Upon embarking on their trip back home, they thought the child was with them somewhere within the flock. One full day had passed before they realized Jesus was not with them!

It took Mary and Joseph three days to finally find Jesus again. He was casually talking to the elders in the temple courtyard. Luke states:

> He was sitting among the teachers, listening to them, and asking them questions. His understanding and his answers stunned everyone who heard him. When his parents saw him, they were shocked. His mother asked him, "Son, why have

you done this to us? Your father and I have been worried sick looking for you!" Jesus said to them, "Why were you looking for me? Didn't you realize that I had to be in my Father's house?"

None of the Gospels recount any other part of Jesus' childhood. The next chapter in his amazing journey takes us directly to his baptism in which his cousin John is the main character.

Preparation for What Was to Come

The act of baptism is an essential Christian rite, although it does have roots in other ancient traditions. The Jewish *tevilah*, for example, basically consists of a purification ritual where a person's entire body is immersed in water inside a stepped pool called a *mikveh*. During the earliest times of Christianity, baptism by immersion was quite regular, but later on, the most common way to baptize people became the affusion, where water would be poured on the head of the person being baptized.

Even though both the Jewish *tevilah* and the Christian baptism are similar in form, they have divergent objectives. Jewish laws require ritual baths on a regular basis; for instance, when a woman is about to give birth or to become ritually clean in order to enter the temple. Baptism, for its part, went on to become one of the seven sacraments meant to cleanse humans from the original sin they all carry since their expulsion from the Garden of Eden, as well as to invoke the power of the Trinity. It is only done once during the believer's lifetime.

When John, who is considered one of the forerunners of Christianity, started performing his immersion rituals, he emphasized the need to repent of bad deeds. He apparently "told people about a baptism of repentance for the forgiveness of sins" (Luke 3:3).

The encounter between Jesus and his cousin John is portrayed in all four Gospels. This very well-respected son of the priest Zechariah was attracting large crowds of people, and he became so famous with his preaching and ritual baptisms that people started wondering if he might, in fact, be the Messiah. John responded to these people, "I baptize you with water. But the one who is more powerful than I is coming. I am not worthy to untie his sandal straps. He will baptize you with the Holy Spirit and fire" (Luke 3:16).

When Jesus came to John, the Gospels relate that the skies opened, and a dove came down representing the Holy Spirit. Then a voice from heaven was heard saying this man being baptized was his son.

Matthew states that after being baptized, Jesus Christ told his followers to "make disciples of all nations, baptizing them in the name of the Father and of the Son and of the Holy Spirit" (Matthew 28:19-20)—hence, the incorporation of this phrase in every Christian baptism.

During the first centuries of Christianity, baptisms were mostly performed on adults. The majority of people to this new religion were Greco-Roman pagans, so it was not until after the second century that the baptism of children became the norm.

John the Baptist was definitely quite the character, leading a dramatic life and facing a terrible death. He led an ascetic life, which he had learned during his years in the desert alongside monastic communities, such as the strict Essene sect, and some hermits. According to Mark, he had a peculiar diet of locusts and wild honey, and his clothes were made of camel hair. He must have been quite a sight to see, even back then. John was killed by Herod's son, Herod Antipas, due to his outcry regarding the king's illegal betrothal to his half-brother's former wife. This criticism had John jailed and then beheaded later.

John's influence is enormous. Islam also sees him as one of the prophets, mentioning him and his father Zechariah extensively in their holy book, the Qur'an. He is also mentioned by Flavius Josephus in his *Antiquities of the Jews* where he basically reflects on John's relationship to Herod Antipas.

After his encounter and baptism with John, Jesus went on to spend over a month fasting in the Judean desert, probably influenced by his cousin's own experience in this barren land. The span of time he chose to be there—forty days—is numerologically significant as it recalls several important passages in the Bible. This was the same number of days Moses fasted on Mount Zion, and the Israelites had spent forty years roaming barren lands before they arrived at the Promised Land "of Milk and Honey" that God had promised Abraham, which was located "from the River of Egypt to the great river, the River Euphrates" (Genesis 15:18). There has always been a controversy over if this "River of Egypt" is in fact the Nile itself or a brook south of Gaza.

Some accounts state that this journey into the desert took Jesus as far away as India or Tibet, where he could have learned many healing methods and some principles he implemented later on which are akin to Buddhist ideals.

Jesus' experience in the desert had a great impact on him. Many imply it gave him the strength and resolve he needed in order to start his ministry afterward. Only the synoptic Gospels talk about this period of Jesus' life. They state that he was prompted by the devil to sin on three occasions, which Christians refer to as the Temptations of Christ.

First of all, after Jesus started to starve, the devil encouraged him to turn a stone into bread—this was the first temptation. He then offered Jesus to rule over all the kingdoms if he relented into worshiping him. "I will give you all the power and glory of these kingdoms. All of it has been given to me, and I give it to anyone I please. So if you will worship me, all this will be yours," he said, according to the Gospel of Luke (Luke 4:6-7). This was the second temptation. In Jesus' third trial, the devil tried to get him to use his influence as the son of God by tempting him to jump from the top of the temple because his father would come down from heaven to save him anyway.

Each time the devil tempted Jesus Christ, he refused to sway. It is interesting to note that Jesus cited the Book of Deuteronomy, one of the books in the Torah which became the Old Testament's fifth book, in each rebuff he made. This attests to his strict following of the Jewish laws.

After failing to lure Jesus toward him, the devil finally gave up. It was time for Jesus to go back to Nazareth. According to Luke, he was about thirty years old at the time.

Becoming a Miracle-Maker and Healer

Jesus Christ's first shot at becoming a minister, or Messiah, was unsuccessful. He was not very welcome in his hometown, so he decided to roam other localities in the Galilean region. Soon enough, he started gathering followers though. "Come, follow me! I will teach you how to catch people instead of fish," he told two fishermen, Andrew and Simon. These men, who were also brothers, went on to become the first two of Jesus' twelve disciples, also known as the Twelve Apostles, who were Jesus' closest followers and the primary teachers of his messages.

Strong and passionate assertions, like the one he blurted out to Andrew and Simon, were part of Jesus' appeal and helped him to start to garner his fame as a preacher. It is important to note that he never called himself by the term Messiah.

Andrew and Simon were Hellenized Jews, hence the mixed origin of their respective names. Andrew stems from the Greek name *Andreas*, related to the term *andros*, or man. Simon is an Aramaic name, although he became Peter later on. Jesus saw Simon as a fundamental pillar of his ministry, telling him that he would be the rock of his church. This new choice of the name Peter stemmed from playing on the terms *Petros* and *petra*, respectively meaning "Peter" and "rock" in Greek, and which in Hebrew can be translated as "pebble." Anyhow, in the Gospel of Matthew, this change of name is revealed in a somewhat confusing set of words: "Simon, son of Jonah, you are blessed! No human revealed this to you, but my

Father in heaven revealed it to you. You are Peter, and I can guarantee that on this rock I will build my church…I will give you the keys of the kingdom of heaven." We can see here how important this disciple was to Jesus. As a matter of fact, he went on to become the first Patriarch of Antioch and the first Bishop of Rome, which was the heart of the empire. In any case, Peter is considered a "rock" on which the institution of the church was built. The Vatican, Catholicism's capital nowadays, accordingly named its papal basilica as Saint Peter.

Peter (many times also called Simon Peter) and Andrew, together with two other siblings, James and John—also fishermen—became an important quartet among the group of twelve disciples that accompanied Jesus in his travels. The other eight were Philip, Bartholomew, Matthew (referred to as Levi in the Gospels), Thomas, James, Thaddeus (or Judas), Simon the Cananaean (or the Zealot), and Judas Iscariot.

One of Jesus Christ's most iconic miracles, turning water into wine, is not mentioned in the synoptic Gospels; instead, it is only mentioned by John. He recounts that Jesus, his mother, and the disciples had been invited to a wedding in the Galilean town of Cana. Once there, Mary tells her son that the host had run out of wine, to which he answered, "Oh Woman, what has this to do with me? My hour has not yet come." (This moment in Jesus' life was still early on in his ministry, so he was not famous yet.) Mary, nevertheless, tells the servants to obey Jesus' instructions and fill the containers with water and then to take out a glass and bring it to the chief waiter. This man was amazed at what he drank, going to the bridegroom to comment on how "everyone serves the best wine first. When people are drunk, the host serves cheap wine. But you have saved the best wine for now" (John 2:10). This was Jesus' first public miracle.

From then on, the fame of Jesus as a miracle-maker and a healer started growing to impressive proportions throughout Galilee and even all the way to Syria.

People brought him everyone who was sick, those who suffered from any kind of disease or pain. They also brought epileptics, those who were paralyzed, and people possessed by demons [including a boy and several mute people] and he cured them all. Large crowds followed him. They came from Galilee, the Ten Cities, Jerusalem, Judea, and from across the Jordan River. (Matt. 4:24-25)

The Gospels describe how Jesus healed a "serious skin disease," which was probably leprosy, restored the eyesight to several men, and healed a woman who had been bleeding for twelve years. Jesus never requested or received payments for any of these deeds. The miracles started mounting at the same rhythm as his fame.

New Ideas Are Heard

Jesus also became widely known for his impactful speeches filled with teachings that were looked upon as quite revolutionary for his time. His longest, and some might say the most famous of all, is the Sermon on the Mount. Only Matthew documented it in his Gospel. By this time, Jesus had already acquired a solid following, so when he saw a large crowd gathering around him, he decided to go up a mountain to speak to them from above. There is a general agreement that the most likely location for this sermon was a hill that stretches up from the northwestern shore of Lake Gennesaret in Galilee which has a great acoustic setting. It is nowadays known as the Mount of Beatitudes.

What is so relevant about the Sermon on the Mount, though? Most scholars and theologians agree that it determined much of the basis for Christianity's ethics and moral principles and that it was filled with a deeply spiritual desire for compassion. It also contains the core of what was to become the Christians' beloved prayer Lord's Prayer (also known as Our Father), which millions recite on a daily basis and at every Mass.

Jesus basically reinterpreted Old Testament codes of conduct, yet the way in which he repackaged them moved people and shook their preset beliefs.

The sum of Jesus' teachings in his Sermon on the Mount is what has become known as the Beatitudes, eight blessings spelled out in a proverb-like style. The word was coined from the Greek *beati*, meaning "happy" or "blessed," and they are highly peaceful in their meaning: "Blessed are those who mourn. They will be comforted...Blessed are the merciful, for they shall obtain mercy...Blessed are those who make peace. They will be called God's children," and so on. Luke states that Jesus also recited four of these blessings in his Sermon on the Plain.

Renown fifth-century Christian philosopher Saint Augustine of Hippo (modern-day Algeria) wrote in his widely-read *Commentary on the Sermon on the Mount* that "anyone who piously and earnestly ponders the Sermon on the Mount...I believe he will find therein...the perfect standard of the Christian Life." In sum, one could find the supreme embodiment of Christianity's moral theology in this sermon.

Italian thirteenth-century philosopher and theologian Saint Thomas Aquinas went even further, defining the Beatitudes as "perfect works emanating from virtues perfected by the gifts" of the Holy Spirit. This way, the Sermon on the Mount is linked to one of Isaiah's prophecies stating that "the spirit of the Lord shall rest upon him [the Messiah], the spirit of wisdom and understanding, the spirit of counsel and might, the spirit of knowledge and the fear of the Lord" (Isaiah 11:2-3).

Other innovative teachings that set Jesus apart were the ways in which he talked about controlling anger, dealing with sexuality, the importance of being honest, and overcoming hate in order to transform it into unconditional love, among other spiritual topics.

According to the Gospel of Matthew, Jesus Christ states:

You have heard that it was said, "An eye for an eye and a tooth for a tooth." But I tell you not to oppose an evil person. If someone slaps you on your right cheek, turn your other cheek to him as well. If someone wants to sue you in order to take your shirt, let him have your coat too. If someone forces you to go one mile, go two miles with him...You have heard that it was said, "Love your neighbor, and hate your enemy." But I tell you this: Love your enemies, and pray for those who persecute you. (Matt. 5:38-44)

This particular passage includes some of Christianity's most prominent lessons: turn the other cheek and love others as you love yourself. Luke also offers a similar version of these teachings in his Gospel.

Throughout different parts of Israel, miracles continued to be performed and teachings were set like brazen fire within many minds. On two occasions, Jesus decided to multiply the food to give to the people. All four Gospels talk about the first instance when he was able to feed five thousand people from the meager portions a boy had given him. John recounts that "taking the five loaves and the two fish, he looked up to heaven, and blessed and broke them, and gave them to the disciples to set before the crowd. And all ate and were filled. What was left over was gathered up, twelve baskets of broken pieces" (John 6:11).

In the second instance when Jesus performed a similar miracle, which is only mentioned in the Gospels of Mark and Matthew, he managed to feed a large crowd of four thousand people who had been staying with him for three days and "had nothing to eat."

These miracles, in particular because of the sheer grandiosity of their achievement, created even more acclaim toward the figure of Christ and his immense powers. The symbolic gesture it conveyed—that the Lord will always look after his herd—was very powerful.

As soon as Jesus started increasing his fame across Judea, it was inevitable for him to also begin accumulating enemies. He had been "stepping on too many toes" due to his unorthodox view of the scriptures and due to some of his preaching, which criticized some of the set ways of his time, especially those regarding some of the highly influential priests within the Jewish community.

At one point, people from the Sect of the Pharisees had come from Jerusalem to meet Jesus. The Pharisees, who were very strict followers of ancient Jewish religious standards, saw that some of his disciples did not follow the traditional standards of cleanliness, so they started criticizing them. Jesus did not like this at all and went against the Pharisees with harsh words. "Why do you break the commandment of God because of your traditions?…What goes into a person's mouth does not make him unclean. It is what comes out of the mouth that makes a person unclean," he told all of those present. This was not the only disagreeable encounter with the Pharisees, as the Gospels describe other instances in which this Jewish group definitely displayed their disdain for Jesus.

Jesus continued on his travels and preaching with a series of impacting miracles. He walked over water, cured more sick people, cleaned men who were possessed by demons, and even resurrected people from death. On one occasion, he revived the son of a grieving widow who only had that child and no one else. Jesus went up to the coffin and said, "Young man, I am telling you to come back to life!" (Luke 7:14). The child immediately stood up and began talking. Everyone was amazed.

Perhaps the most famous case of Jesus bringing a person back to life was that of Lazarus. According to the Gospel of John, this man had already been dead for four days when Jesus heard about his situation. Jesus was very close to his sisters, Martha and Mary of Bethany, and promised to help. When he arrived at the rock behind which Lazarus had been buried, Jesus ordered to have the stone taken away. Before doing anything else, he first looked into heaven and said, "Father, I thank you for hearing me. I have known that you always hear me. However, I have said this so that the crowd standing around me will believe that you sent me" (John 11:41-42). He then told Lazarus to come out.

Everyone was amazed at this impressive miracle, which only took Jesus' fame to new heights, although it also brought more animosity against him. Some chief priests and the Pharisees met to discuss what could be done about this man, this trouble-maker who they saw as becoming increasingly dangerous. "If we let him continue what he is doing, everyone will believe in him. Then the Romans will take away our position and our nation," John reports them saying during their meeting. He also states in his Gospel that it was at this moment when they started plotting Jesus' death. The Council, which was a court integrated by relevant members of the Jewish community, ordered to have him arrested once they found out his whereabouts, which would happen during the next Passover.

Another important aspect of Jesus' ministry touched more on the spiritual healing of many who came to meet him. A Pharisee invited Jesus to eat at his house (not all had decided to be his enemy), and when they were at the table, a woman known to be sinful came to him and asked for forgiveness. Luke relates that "she took a bottle of perfume and knelt at his feet. She was crying and washed his feet with her tears. Then she dried his feet with her hair, kissed them over and over again, and poured the perfume on them."

The Pharisee was horrified that Jesus was letting this "sinful" woman touch him. So, he decided to teach the Pharisee a lesson by not even speaking to him directly, instead talking to his disciple Peter—this would have denoted his disdain toward the Pharisee. Jesus asked Peter, "Two men owed a moneylender some money. One owed him five hundred silver coins, and the other owed him fifty. When they could not pay it back, he was kind enough to cancel their debts. Now, who do you think will love him the most?" Peter answered, "I suppose the one who had the largest debt canceled." Jesus answered, "You are right!" (Luke 7:41-43).

With this simple yet forceful story, Jesus taught everything he needed to tell the Pharisee—that everyone has sinned, but this woman, who had asked for special forgiveness, would be the one to most appreciate the fact that Jesus pardoned her more than any other person. "Your faith has saved you. Go in peace!" (Luke 7:50).

The most famous example of Jesus' ministry regarding the pardoning of sins is, without any doubt, the one with Mary Magdalene. All the canonical Gospels name this woman—a total of twelve times, more than any other disciple—which attests to the great importance she had in Jesus' life. "The whole history of western civilization is epitomized in the cult of Mary Magdalene. For many centuries the most obsessively revered of saints, this woman became the embodiment of Christian devotion, which was defined as repentance," states American historian, journalist, and former priest James Carroll.[viii] And this is a fundamental concept around Christianity: If one repents of their sins, one would be forgiven and able to enter the kingdom of God, a.k.a., heaven.

But who was this mysterious woman so present in Jesus' passion, crucifixion, and resurrection? Magdalene was not a part of Mary's name, but it was rather the place she came from: the Galilean fishing town of Magdala.

Luke is the only one to mention her before Jesus' death. He identifies Mary Magdalene as a part of a group of women accompanying Jesus in his travels and "from whom seven demons had gone out" (Luke 8:2). But what were those "demons" she had? There is no reference to their nature in any of the Gospels, and the word can have many interpretations depending on if it is looked from a Hebrew or Gentile point of view. There have been claims that she was a prostitute, a woman with a "carefree" lifestyle. No one knows for sure, but it is known that she was an important person in Jesus' life, a trusted companion, and a disciple. Many speculate that she could have even been his wife, although none of the Gospels hint at this assertion; however, they do place her in a prominent position, which is where the argument of her being his wife stems from.

The historical male views that prevailed in most cultures is perhaps what drove Pope Gregory the Great to declare Mary Magdalene a prostitute in the sixth century. "There are many scholars who argue that because Jesus empowered women to such an extent early in his ministry, it made some of the men who would lead the early church later on uncomfortable," Robert Cargill, editor at *Biblical Archaeology Review*, argues. "And so there were two responses to this. One was to turn her into a prostitute."

Mary would be mostly set aside until 1969 when the Catholic Church conceded that there was not one mention in the Bible that could attest to the fact that she was a prostitute. Mary Magdalene is officially a saint today. She represents a part of the advanced nature of Jesus' preaching and way of life. It was not common to see women as disciples of any kind during that time, so to be held in such a well-respected way by Jesus and to have a prominent position at certain moments in his life, was a significant symbol of female empowerment back then.

Mary Magdalene is widely named in other noncanonical scriptures, such as the Gnostic Gospels, a group of second- and third-century CE papyrus codices that were found in Egypt in the year 1945. They are also called the Nag Hammadi library for the nearby town where they were discovered. Some of these documents are Christian (although not officially recognized as canonical), and others have a more agnostic nature. They include texts like the gospels of Philip and Thomas, the Prayer of the Apostle Paul, and the Exegesis of the Soul, among others, which amount to up to one hundred books and excerpts of two others.

Passion and Death

Jesus predicted what would happen to him, how he would die, and that he would be resurrected. He spoke to his disciples about his fate and that he would return to life—not just once, but three times.

The last time he touched upon the subject was right before entering Jerusalem, taking his disciples apart and saying, "The Son of Man will be betrayed to the chief priests and the experts in Moses' Teachings. They will condemn him to death and hand him over to foreigners. They will make fun of him, whip him, and crucify him. But on the third day, he will be brought back to life" (Matt. 20:17-19). This, of course, shook the disciples once again, as it had done when he first mentioned this, and they still could not take these words seriously until the inevitable happened.

There is also information on Jesus' fate in the Old Testament. Isaiah had prophesied why and how this Messiah would be killed, stating that "he was despised and rejected by men…he was wounded for our transgressions, he was bruised for our iniquities: the chastisement of our peace was upon him" (Isaiah 53:3). In the Christian faith, Jesus did not sin at any time; he simply took on humanity's sins, and those were the ones he was "punished" for. He sacrificed himself in order to save humankind. This idea is essential to understanding Christianity's core.

Before falling in disgrace, Jesus Christ's entrance into Jerusalem— the capital of the Jewish province, hence its importance as a crucial place for him to continue spreading his word—was that of a king. On the eve of Passover, a large crowd came to the road to meet him. He was hailed by the people who started chanting, "Hosanna to the Son of David! Blessed is the one who comes in the name of the Lord! Hosanna in the highest heaven!" This phrase is crucial in many aspects. Jesus is greeted with "Hosanna," a word of worship which refers, in both the Hebrew and Aramaic languages, to the concept of "rescue," to someone who is a "savior."

Both Jews and Christians regularly use the "Hosanna" term for ceremonial purposes. Moreover, the entire phrase that the people from Jerusalem chanted at Jesus is nowadays included in every liturgical Mass.

Another symbolic aspect of that day relates to the fact that those who had come to see Jesus' triumphant arrival in Jerusalem carried palm branches with them. In ancient times, these were a symbol of eternal life, well-being, and victory. In countries around the world, people make crosses and other crafts out of palm branches after they have been blessed by a priest. In places where this type of tree is not available, it is customary to substitute palms for pussy willow, box, yew, or olive branches. Christians incorporated the palm branch as a symbol and made a tradition out of it by giving out palm branches on Palm Sunday. This day commemorates when Jesus was received like a king in Jerusalem, and it is held one week before Easter, which is the day that celebrates Jesus' resurrection. Palm Sunday is considered one of the most important festivities in the Christian religious calendar. The events that happened to Jesus on that Sunday were so relevant that they are mentioned in all four Gospels with particular detail.

Jesus did not waste time once he arrived in Jerusalem, and during the days just before Passover, he continued his attacks on the Jewish leaders and Pharisees. Uttering harsh words of criticism, he went on and on about their hypocrisy: "How horrible it will be for you, experts in Moses' Teachings and Pharisees! You hypocrites! You give God one-tenth of your mint, dill, and cumin. But you have neglected justice, mercy, and faithfulness…You clean the outside of cups and dishes. But inside they are full of greed and uncontrolled desires" (Matt. 23:13-26).

The Jewish leaders decided once and for all that they had had enough of this unruly self-proclaimed Messiah and plotted his final demise. Jesus knew these would be some of his last days on Earth, and he started to prepare both himself and those around him for the events to come.

Jesus gathered his disciples around him on the Mount of Olives and issued some last instructions. He predicted the end of times and the birth of a new world, saying, "Not one of these stones will be left on top of another. Each one will be torn down," which alludes to how there will be much commotion on Earth but that afterward, this new kingdom will come.

The disciples asked him what would be the signs indicating the world was about to end. Jesus spoke that there would be terrible events but that these would not signal the end. On the contrary, this "final time" would happen only when the "good news about the kingdom" was spread throughout the world, basically meaning his teachings. Jesus' prediction of the end of times and the eventual coming of the kingdom of heaven is laid out in Matthew 25. It is a stark outlook, but it also predicts a bright future for those Jesus wanted to save, the ones he predicted would be the ones to enter the kingdom of God.

This lengthy chat between Jesus and his disciples took place on the night in which he was to be betrayed. The Jewish patriarchs had already sent out a warrant for his arrest, and a group of people was looking for him. One of the disciples had met with them, stating he knew where Jesus was and that he could take them to him. He said that the one he kissed on the cheek would be the self-proclaimed Messiah.

Jesus and the disciples made preparations to enjoy their Passover meal at a house in the city. When they were all sitting together, Jesus said that he knew who had told of his whereabouts to the chief priests and that he was sitting right there in the room. He also said the sign would be a kiss on the cheek. All of the disciples were aghast, and each one started asking which one of them it could be. One stood out that night—Judas Iscariot. When he asked, "You do not mean me, do you, Rabbi?" Jesus answered, "Yes, I do." He knew beforehand who the traitor was (Matt. 26:25).

During this dinner, which is known as the Last Supper, Jesus gave out a whole set of recommendations and instructions for the disciples to follow in order for his teachings to be spread out to the world. He knew this would be his last night as a free man before his crucifixion the next day. This Passover dinner was a way to seal his commitment with the disciples, to give them the strength they needed in order to continue his legacy, to teach others his doctrine, and to develop his Church. It is at this moment that he established the ritual of the Eucharist, also known as the Holy Communion or the Lord's Supper, a fundamental aspect of Christianity. This rite is performed at every Mass and at other sacramental moments such as the First Communion, Confirmation, and marriage ceremonies.

The three synoptic Gospels, as well as the First Epistle to the Corinthians (another part of the New Testament), state the Eucharist involves two symbols: bread, which symbolizes Jesus Christ's flesh, and wine, which symbolizes his blood. According to Christian doctrine, these epitomize his sacrifice for humanity's sake as the wine and the bread represent his flesh and blood, the flesh and blood of someone who gave his life for the salvation of all the people on Earth.

The Gospels relate the exact words Jesus uttered on that fateful night, words that are repeated like a mantra at every Christian Mass throughout the world. He took the bread and blessed it, then broke it and gave each disciple a piece while saying, "Take this, and eat it. This is my body, which is given up for you. Do this to remember me." Jesus did the same with the wine, taking a cup, saying a prayer of thanksgiving, and then giving it to the disciples. While each one of them sipped on it, Jesus told them, "This is my blood, the blood of the promise. It is poured out for many people so that sins are forgiven."

This scene at the Last Supper became an institution that reminds Christians that the celebration of eating and drinking Jesus' own flesh and blood is an anticipation of the banquet they will enjoy once they gain access to the kingdom of God.

It was after dinner when a crowd carrying sticks and swords came looking for Jesus with Judas Iscariot guiding them. He greeted the Messiah with a kiss on the cheek, and Jesus was immediately arrested and taken away for trial in front of the chief priest, Joseph ben Caiaphas. The rest of the disciples ran away—just as Jesus had predicted—afraid of everything that was happening.

Jesus was sentenced to death by the Jewish Council for "dishonoring God." The chief priests could not stand the fact that Jesus kept saying he was God's son. It was at this moment that his torment started. They stripped Jesus naked, spat on him, and beat him up. He was afterward taken away to meet the Roman prefect of Judea at the time, Pontius Pilate, who felt the accusations against Jesus were largely baseless. Yet the mob was adamant and clamored for him to receive the death sentence.

It did not help that Jesus kept mostly silent during the interrogation. As was customary during Passover, one prisoner was normally pardoned as a gesture of goodwill. There was a criminal—Barabbas, a man that was "in prison with the rebels who had committed murder during the insurrection" against the Romans (Luke 23:19)—who Pilate presented to the crowd, saying he could be the one to face the death sentence instead of Jesus. Even though there are no other historical accounts of this "bandit" (as he is described by John), all four Gospels talk about Jesus' trial. The exalted crowd was adamant though and chose Jesus instead. Luke relates that Jesus was brought to Herod as well, who mocked him (Luke 23:5-16), but none of the three other Gospels mention this encounter.

Pilate gave in to the crowd's demands, although he made it clear that he did not want to be blamed for sending what he saw as an innocent man to his death. So, according to the Gospel of Matthew, Pilate "took some water and washed his hands in front of the crowd," claiming he would not "be guilty of killing this man." This phrase of "washing your hands" became commonly used after that. People use it whenever they want to be cleared of responsibility during a conflict of interest.

So, Barabbas was freed, and the Roman soldiers took Jesus away to execute him. To mock him, they put a red cape on him, sank a crown of thorns on his head, and made him grab a stick as if it were a scepter. "Long live the king of the Jews!" they chanted. The suffering was unimaginable, although the worst was yet to come.

The chosen method for Jesus to die is one of the cruelest and most painful deaths anyone could go through: by being nailed onto a cross. Moreover, Jesus was made to carry his own cross from the Roman governor's palace to Golgotha, known to the Hebrews as the Calvary, which was the place right outside Jerusalem's walls where these crucifixions were performed during that time. Jesus fell once, twice, three times on the way there. The only small act of pity the soldiers allowed him was that at some point on the road, a man called Simon of Cyrene helped him carry the cross during part of the journey.

Crucifixion was regularly used by Persians, Romans, Carthaginians, and Seleucids throughout the sixth century BCE until the fourth century CE when it was abolished within the Roman Empire. Only some scattered instances of crucifixions have happened in modern times. There were reports of Christian girls being crucified during the Armenian Genocide, which was performed by the Ottoman government in 1915, for example.

Jesus was crucified alongside two thieves. The Roman soldiers attached him to the cross with nails in his hands and feet, and Pilate ordered to have a sign made out for him that read, "Jesus from Nazareth, the king of the Jews," written in the four languages used at the time: Hebrew, Aramaic, Latin, and Greek. The inscription normally employed nowadays is the acronym of the phrase in Latin, spelled INRI.

Jesus hung from the cross in agony for practically the whole day. At one moment, he cried out for help, pleading with his father in heaven to relieve him of his suffering. "My God, my God, why have you abandoned me?" he screamed in pain. Right after this wretched plea, Jesus exhaled his last breath. According to the Gospel of John (19:31-37), the soldiers threw a spear at him, which left a gaping hole in one side of his ribcage, to confirm that he was dead. It was customary to break the legs of people being crucified in order to hasten their deaths. When the soldiers saw that Jesus had already passed away, they did not break his. This detail would fulfill a prophecy which stated that none of the Messiah's bones "will be broken and they will look on him whom they pierced" (Zechariah 12:10).

The spear used against Jesus is known by various names, mainly the Holy Lance, the Spear of Longinus (which was supposedly the name of the Roman soldier who threw it, and it is believed that he later converted to Christianity), the Holy Spear, and the Lance of Destiny. There are three different relics of the spear still existing nowadays, all claiming to be the original one. The first one rests below the dome of St. Peter's Basilica, the second one is the Hofburg, a palace in Vienna, Austria, and there is a third one in Armenia. The Vatican states that "it was believed that whoever possesses the Holy Spear and understands the powers it serves, holds in his hand the destiny of the world for good or evil. The Holy Spear was and is still a religious relic that most of the Roman Catholics believe struck the side of Christ."[ix] However, there is no way to confirm if any of these lances were used against Jesus.

The synoptic Gospels relate that supernatural events took place right at the time of Jesus' death. All three state that the sky darkened for a few hours, even though it was still daytime, and that the temple's curtains were torn apart. Matthew went a bit further and said that the earth shook, splitting open the surrounding rocks where people were buried and that many came back from the dead at that moment.

Modern geologists have analyzed the varves—annual layers of deposition in the sediments—within the region where Jesus was crucified, confirming that there was indeed an earthquake in the first century somewhere between 26 and 36 CE. Concerning the darkness that descended upon Earth just at the time of Jesus' death, experts agree it could have been a sandstorm.

The only people from Jesus' circle present at the time of his death were the women; the men had all run away. His mother Mary, Mary Magdalene, and another Mary, who was the mother of James and Joseph, as well as a fourth woman according to Matthew, were all at the foot of the cross. Once again, we see here the dignified place women have in this story—one of endurance, faith, and honor.

After Pilate gave the order, the women received Jesus' body for burial. They placed him in a tomb and put a large rock in front of it.

Coming Back to Life

Three days had passed after Jesus was buried, and once again, the women played a relevant role in this poignant tale. They had decided to visit Jesus' grave and saw that the heavy rock sealing the entrance had been removed. Jesus' body was nowhere to be found. They were shocked, wondering what could have happened. It is important to note that these were days filled with emotion and tension for all those in Jesus' circle. They were being persecuted and harassed, and this situation regarding his tomb was, at least on the surface, not a good sign.

But then an angel appeared to the women and told them that Jesus Christ had been resurrected. "Do not be afraid! I know you are looking for Jesus, who was crucified. He is not here. He has been brought back to life," he said (Matt. 28:5-6). The Gospels describe how they ran back to the disciples to announce that his body was not there anymore and what the angel had told them.

The Gospels of Matthew, Mark, and John relate that Jesus made a few appearances before going back to heaven. He first made himself visible to Mary Magdalene. Again, it is worth noting that he chose a woman to first give direct news of his resurrection.

Jesus then appeared to the disciples in different instances. One of them, Thomas, had not been present yet to see Jesus and was in disbelief at the story of his resurrection. "I refuse to believe this unless I see the nail marks in his hands, put my fingers into them, and put my hand into his side," he said, according to the Gospel of John. So, on another day, Jesus appeared in front of the whole group, even though they were behind closed doors. He went up to Thomas and told him, "Put your finger here, and look at my hands. Take your hand, and put it into my side. Stop doubting, and believe."

Thomas started believing in Jesus' return to life, but the Messiah scolded him, stating that his faith was "because you have seen me. Blessed are those who have not seen me but believe" (John 20:27-29). This was an important lesson Jesus wanted to give his disciples: the importance of believing beyond physical proof. He wanted to spread this fundamental idea among all human beings.

This exchange between Jesus and Thomas has become a particularly famous passage from the New Testament, from which the much-used "Doubting Thomas" and "Seeing and believing like Saint Thomas" phrases come from.

The third time Jesus appeared to his disciples, he had a special conversation with them, instructing them to spread his teachings across the world. "Wherever you go, make disciples of all nations: Baptize them in the name of the Father, and of the Son, and of the Holy Spirit. Teach them to do everything I have commanded you. And remember that I am always with you until the end of time" (Matt. 28:19-20). He then ascended into heaven.

The concept of people coming back from the dead was not new in Jewish culture. British historian Peter Watson believes "the idea of the resurrection probably appeared for the first time towards the year 160 BCE during the period of religious martyrdom, and precisely as a response to it (how could it be possible that martyrs would die forever?)" The first time we see it mentioned is in the Book of Daniel, and since it concurs with the Zoroastrian idea of heaven and earth, which the Jewish people adopted during their exile in Babylon, Watson asserts that "with the resurrection the same could have happened, also being another Zoroastrian idea."

During his lifetime, Jesus was known as Jesus of Galilee or Jesus of Nazareth, as the custom back then was to identify people with their place of birth or residence. It was only after his death that the word *Christ* started being used. This word is derived from the Greek

Christos, basically meaning *Meshiah* or Messiah, the Hebrew word for "the anointed one." From then on, "Christ" became a sort of title for Jesus, and it has been used in different ways. The Apostle Paul included both "Jesus Christ" and "Christ Jesus" (Romans 1:1; 3:24) in his letters, as well as by itself, simply referring to him as "Christ" (Romans 5:6).

Week of Utmost Importance

Jesus' last magnificent arrival in Jerusalem, the quarrel with the chief priests, the Last Supper and conversations with his disciples, and his ensuing torture, death, and resurrection is what is called the Passion in Christianity. The events before Easter, the day that celebrates Jesus coming back to life, form a part of the most important religious ceremonial festivity for Christians: The Holy Week.

Throughout seven days, which always fall between March and April depending on the year, Christians commemorate everything that happened during that fateful period of time. Every day has a name, and a series of events of the utmost importance is performed.

The first day of the Holy Week, Palm Sunday, is one of celebration. Then, depending on the region, some Christian denominations reserve special rites for Holy Monday and Holy Tuesday, as well as for what is called Spy Wednesday, which was when Judas plotted to deliver Jesus to the priests. Orthodox churches celebrate these days more than Catholics. On Maundy or Holy Thursday, the day of Jesus' last dinner with his disciples, some Christians observe the custom to visit "the seven temples" or seven churches in their area. The word Maundy means "command" in Latin, and it refers to Jesus ordering the disciples during the Last Supper to love and serve one another. Good Friday—which marks the day when Jesus was sentenced, made to carry his cross and died—is a day of sorrow, with people normally performing strict penance, fasting and repentance. On Holy Saturday, also called Easter Vigil, people rest, neither mourning nor rejoicing.

It is on Easter Sunday that Christians celebrate again, and it is perhaps the most joyful day of the year for them. Jesus came back to life on this day, which would be a cause for celebration, of course. There are a whole series of events and traditions—some religious, others more secular in spirit—that take place on this day of the year. People go to Mass in a joyous gathering. The fabled "Easter Bunny" places eggs in children's gardens—originally, they were real ones, but now they are made of chocolate—who then embark on fun egg-hunting sprees.

But why a bunny? What has that got to do with Christianity? Again, we find here elements of pagan customs assimilated to Christian festivities. At about the same period as Passover and Easter, many pre-Christian Anglo-Saxon communities paid homage to the goddess Eastre, who represented springtime and fertility. Her symbol was—you guessed right—a rabbit. This very fertile animal mostly breeds during this time of the year. They epitomize new life, which is a concept that relates very well to the significance of the Holy Week. Many languages of Anglo-Saxon origin adapted the goddess' name of Eastre to refer to the Holy Week—Easter in English and Ostern in German, for example. Other scholars have also found that Mary was associated with rabbits in many medieval scriptures and paintings, most likely due to the belief of Greek origin that these animals could reproduce while still being virginal.

The Holy Week festivities have changed over the centuries. Many customs have come and gone on this special occasion. Originally, only Good Friday and Holy Saturday were observed. It was in the fourth century that the term Holy Week was coined, and other days then started to be added to the holy festivities calendar, with Easter Sunday being celebrated as a joyous occasion once the week ended.

Chapter 3 – Early Church

Most of what we know about Jesus' conception, birth, early childhood, adult life, martyrdom, death, and eventual resurrection comes from the four Gospels, the main part of the New Testament written by Luke, Mark, Matthew, and John, who were also known as the Four Evangelists. The word "gospel" derives from *godspell*, an Anglo-Saxon translation of the Latin word *evangelium*, which means "good news."

Apart from the prophecies stated within Jewish tradition, these Evangelists decided to write their own accounts on his life, as well as the aspects regarding his death and what he meant to humanity in general. Each did so in their own way, starting around forty years after Jesus Christ's death and continuing to around 100 CE.

Mark was most surely the first Evangelist to write about Jesus' life. The majority of scholars agree that he was born in Cyrene, present-day Libya. There is no information on the date of his birth, although his death can be traced to the year 68 CE. After writing his Gospel, somewhere around the year 65 CE, Mark went on to live in Egypt, where he established the Church of Alexandria, thus being honored nowadays as the founder of Christianity in Africa. His relevance is such that the Coptic Orthodox and Catholic Churches, as well as the Greek Orthodox Church of Alexandria, all claim to descend directly from the original community Mark created in the first century CE.

Like most original promoters of the Christian faith, he died in martyrdom, dragged by horses through the streets of Alexandria.

Most scholars state that Luke was a Greek physician and that he was the only Gentile of the Evangelists. Others, nonetheless, think he could have also been a Hellenic Jew from Antioch, where there was a flourishing community of people combining Jewish religious traditions with elements of Greek culture. There is a strong consensus that Luke's account was the second Gospel to be written, around 85 CE. It is also the longest.

Both Matthew and John knew Jesus personally, being two of the twelve original disciples who accompanied him during the last part of his life. Matthew's Gospel was probably written between 85 and 90 CE. He also suffered martyrdom, dying in Ethiopia from a sword wound.

John was the youngest of the disciples, and his Gospel was the last to be written, probably around 95-100 CE. He is the only one of the Evangelists to die from old age, although not before suffering oppression as well. He miraculously escaped from being boiled in oil during his persecution in Rome. Afterward, he served time at the prison island of Patmos, where he wrote the Book of Revelations. After being set free, John went on to become the Bishop of Edessa, passing away at the approximate age of one hundred.

All of the Gospels were probably originally written in Greek; at least, the oldest known manuscripts known to us were written in this language. However, some scholars argue that they may have been written in Aramaic, the language used in Israel at the time. There is no clear evidence to confirm or deny this argument. Very early translations in Latin, Syrian, and Egyptian—some as early as the year 200 CE—have survived to the modern day. Famed archaeologist and New Testament scholar Carsten Peter Thiede has asserted that as far back as 66 CE, the Gospel of Matthew had already been distributed in Egypt, so it is logical to assume that at least this Gospel in particular was already in Greek by then, the predominant language that would have been understood by almost everyone during that time.

Apart from the four Gospels, the New Testament also consists of other texts: The Acts of the Apostles, the Epistles (which are basically letters), and the Book of Revelations. When the Christian Church started suffering due to its several divisions between the East and West, its content, as well as several other doctrinal principles, would vary slightly.

Christianity, as a new religion, started developing in the Middle East shortly after Jesus' death, mainly in the Roman province of Judea at first. These early adherents of Jesus' teachings, rising after approximately 33 CE, were Jews, led by the disciples, who were now considered apostles.

At what time did they change from disciples to apostles? Jesus had many disciples, or pupils, not only the twelve that were closest to him. At the beginning of his ministry when he started his preaching throughout Galilee and the rest of the Judean province, everyone was a disciple, as they were all learning. But toward the end of Jesus' life on Earth, he needed to specially instruct those he chose as the wisest, the ones more adept to carry on with the torch of his knowledge.

These chosen disciples were no longer students but "carriers" of a new message. At that moment, Jesus changes their status. "He called together all of his disciples and chose twelve of them to be apostles. Here are their names: Simon (whom he named Peter), Andrew (Peter's brother), James, John, Philip, Bartholomew, Matthew, Thomas, James (son of Alpheus), Simon (who was called the zealot), Judas (son of James), Judas Iscariot (who later betrayed him)" (Luke 6:13-16).

After Judas Iscariot double-crossed Jesus, he was so guilt-stricken that he committed suicide soon after Jesus' death. So, with Judas Iscariot out of the way, Matthias was incorporated into this recently elected group of "carriers" of the new truth.

The word apostle comes from the Greek word *apóstolos*, which means "one who is sent off" or "to send out." These apostles would be delivering Christ's message to the people. In the beginning, the idea was to place Jesus as the Messiah the Jewish people had been waiting for so long, yet this was not to become widely accepted within the general population.

That part of the first century, somewhere between 33 and 100 CE, is known as the Apostolic Age basically due to the work and relevance those apostles had in establishing the Christian faith, as well as building some of the first Church government institutions. The end of this era came about when the last one of them died, which was John in approximately around the year 96 CE. This was a period of special significance for Christians since the people who had personal contact with Jesus were still alive.

This Apostolic Age was characterized by intense missionary activity on behalf of those first apostles and many others who adhered to Christ's teachings early on, even though they never knew Jesus in person. This was the case of Paul; Cornelius, who is said to be the first Gentile to be baptized as a Christian (remember that the first Christians were all Jews); and Saint Matthias, among others. These missionary efforts during the Apostolic Age extended throughout Asia Minor, Greece, Macedonia, Persia, Rome, and even Spain.

There is one particularly important day that surged during the Apostolic Age called Pentecost. This traditional holiday is celebrated fifty days after Easter Sunday and marks the day when the Holy Spirit descended upon the apostles and about a hundred other early followers of Jesus Christ. These men were all supposedly gathered in an upper room called the Cenacle, in a building that—according to tradition—still exists to this day. It is believed to be within David's Tomb in Jerusalem. Nevertheless, there is no conclusive evidence that this specific place was the actual Cenacle used during the first Pentecost.

The Cenacle is considered to be the first Christian Church. The apostles and other early adherents of the Christian faith apparently used this place to gather and talk about their newfound ideals. Some even think that it was the same room where the Last Supper was held.

Pentecost is celebrated by all branches of Christianity but in different ways. For example, it is a solemn act for Catholics, while Pentecost is considered one of the Great Feasts of the Eastern Orthodox Church. On their part, the Anglicans call this day White Sunday, Whitsunday, or simply Whitsun.

Even though Christianity originated and grew in the eastern part of the Roman Empire, it established strong roots in the western realms soon after. Yet it was in the Mediterranean city of Antioch, in what is now southeastern Turkey, that this "sect" was first called "Christians," meaning "followers of Christ" in Greek. One of the apostles, Paul, established his headquarters there somewhere around 47 to 55 CE. This man—formerly named Saul of Tarsus, who followed the Jewish faith and was also a Roman citizen—was not a part of the— original circle that followed Jesus during his lifetime. On the contrary, he persecuted these "rebels" in the area of Jerusalem, who he believed were looking to subvert the established order within society. That is until Jesus appeared to him.

The Acts of the Apostles relates that while Saul was looking out "to arrest any man or woman who followed the way of Christ and imprison them in Jerusalem," he saw a sudden bright ray of light coming down from heaven and heard a voice asking "Why are you persecuting me?" He asked who this voice was, and the answer was "Jesus." After this episode, Saul was blinded for three days until a man named Ananias came to his rescue.

Ananias had been ordered by Jesus to meet the blinded Saul and to place his hands on his face. He was puzzled, being aware of the terrible way in which this man persecuted Christians. But Jesus insisted. "Go! I have chosen this man to bring my name to nations, to kings, and to the people of Israel. I will show him how much he has to suffer for the sake of my name" (Acts 9:1-22).

As soon as Ananias did what he was told, Saul recovered his vision. Saul, from then on, became a fervent follower of Christ and would go on to assume one of the Church's most relevant positions in this turbulent first century for Christians. His conversion happened very early on after Jesus had died, estimated between the years 31 and 36 CE.

It was common for Jewish people who also had Roman citizenship, such as Saul's family, to have two names—one of Hebrew origin and another with a more Roman meaning. Such was the case with Saul, whose other name was Paul. "After his conversion, Saul determined to bring the gospel to the Gentiles, so he dusted off his Roman name and became known as Paul, a name Gentiles were accustomed to...Adopting his Roman name was typical of Paul's missionary style. His method was to put people at their ease and to approach them with his message in a language and style they could relate to."[x]

Paul was essential in deciding that Christ's gospel was not to be confined to the Jewish people only but that it could also be taught among non-Jews, or Gentiles. The Hellenic world in which Jesus Christ's teachings kept expanding became a key tool for Paul to transform Christianity into an institution. Both Greek culture and Roman law elements—those classical worldviews which helped shape the Western world—were eventually molded together with this new "Christian truth" that was being told. Many Jews would go on to follow this novel path, but people of different backgrounds from all over the empire also started coming together, captivated by Jesus Christ and his teachings.

Thus, Christianity continued spreading like wildfire across different communities. This could be seen as the spark which started separating Christianity from Judaism in both their forms and structure.

Paul also provides important information regarding Jesus' ministry, mainly through his letters, or the so-called Epistles. Most of the ones included in the New Testament are from him. Those attributed to Paul's authorship are Romans, Corinthians I and II, Galatians, Ephesians, Philippians, Colossians, Thessalonians I and II, Timothy I and II, Titus and Philemon. There has been some debate if Paul actually wrote all of those letters though. Some scholars believe some were written by his students, especially the last ones. Nevertheless, they were definitely created before the Gospels.

The apostles continued to spread Jesus' messages on missionary journeys throughout the known world at the time, and it is fair to say that they took their mission quite seriously with a passion that bore fruit. Among other regions, they went into Syria, North Africa, Egypt, modern-day Turkey, Asia Minor, Greece, Persia, Ethiopia, the Iberian Peninsula, and India—and, of course, to Rome, the epicenter of the Roman Empire.

The great communications network within the Roman Empire was an excellent tool that helped expand this new religion throughout all of its realms. These first Christians were sporadically persecuted at first. Most of the apostles faced gruesome deaths, a product of their newfound belief in Jesus. Peter was crucified upside down in Rome because he said he was not worthy of dying the same way as Jesus. Paul was beheaded, also in the Roman Empire's capital. Others were burned, clubbed, stoned, or stabbed to death. But Christianity's faithful followers eventually persevered, and it was finally adopted as the Roman Empire's only religion after the fourth century.

This oppression of Christians within the Roman Empire is not as extensive or cruel as it has sometimes been portrayed. Emperor Nero did blame them for the Great Fire of Rome of 64 CE that almost completely destroyed the capital, and this is when Paul's and Peter's gruesome deaths happened, along with many other martyrs. But it was after 250 CE that Christians received the most oppression when emperors, such as Decius and Diocletian, exerted a series of persecutions. Under their rule, many Christians were ferociously harassed and killed. But apart from these specific periods, Christians were largely tolerated during the first three centuries CE, mostly living in peace in small and somewhat secretive societies.

Western Roman and Balkan region emperors, Constantine I and Licinius respectively, approved to give Christianity a legal status, under the famous Edict of Milan, in the year 313.

Constantine then went beyond simple tolerance toward Christians. He educated himself on its principles, becoming a catechumen—someone who starts following Christian views without formally becoming one.

During those times, a fight of ideas had ensued between two main opposing views regarding Jesus' religion: Arianism and Nicene Christianity. Arianism promoted the idea that Jesus was the son of God and hence a separate entity in his own right. Nicene Christians, on the other hand, believed that Jesus and God, together with the Holy Spirit, were one and indistinct—the Trinity doctrine in sum. There were also still many within the Roman Empire who did not want to rescind their pagan gods and pre-Christian beliefs. In sum, there was a lot of confusion regarding which codes should be followed and respected as sacred.

It was Constantine the Great—as he was later called—who would preside over the first ecumenical meeting of the Christian Church to discuss many of these conflicts. The entire body of religious leaders got together in 325 at the Council of Nicaea, a region in present-day Turkey, and after extensive deliberations, they established certain principles regarding orthodoxy within the religion. During this encounter, the Arian theology was declared heretical. The Nicene dogma and its Trinity principle would then become the official set of beliefs within the Christian religion.

Constantine would officially be baptized in the Christian faith on his deathbed, becoming the first Roman emperor to do so. Constantine's heirs, his sons Constantius II and Contans, had different views on Christianity, specifically on the issue regarding Jesus' nature.

At some point, Constantine's nephew, Julius, became emperor, and he tried to promote the freedom of religions and cultures but to no avail. Christianity had cut deep within too many Romans.

It would be Theodosius I, also called Theodosius the Great, who would establish Nicene Christianity as the Roman Empire's official state religion in 380 with the Edict of Thessalonica. Romans were already under attack from barbarian tribes coming from the north and northeast of Europe—Vandals, Ostrogoths, Visigoths, Huns, and Taifals, among others. Upon his death, the Roman Empire was permanently divided into two (it had been split before in previous centuries as well). The eastern domain went to Theodosius' oldest son Arcadius, who ruled from Constantinople, and the western realm went to his youngest son Honorius, who ruled from Rome and then later Ravenna.

Christianity Sets Its Canons

The early days of Christianity allowed for all sorts of schools of thought and diverse tendencies within the teachings of Jesus Christ, such as we saw with the case of Arianism and Nicene theology. Apart from the Gospels of Luke, Matthew, Mark, and John, many other texts circulated among the different Christian communities that were surging in the Middle East, the Far East, Rome itself, and North Africa.

It was only after three hundred years after the Gospels were written that what we know as the New Testament was finally put together and set as canonical, meaning these sacred books were officially accepted as genuine. This is a very important turning point in the formation of the Christian institution. The New Testament canon was first presented by Saint Athanasius of Alexandria in a letter, written in 367, to the churches he presided over in Egypt, and it was finally approved in the third and fourth Councils of Carthage, which got together in the years 397 and 419 respectively. These Councils were presided over by none other than Saint Augustine himself, one of the most prominent and influential Christian thinkers of all times.

Throughout the centuries, several rites became sacramental, and Christians consider them to be important religious ceremonies that impart divine grace on the people partaking in them. There are seven in total:

- *Baptism* is, in most cases, performed on babies or young children, although people of any age who are willing to convert must go through this rite in order to formally become a Christian. This sacrament was the first to be practiced since the beginning of the Christian faith.

- The *Eucharist*, or the *Holy Communion*, is the ceremony that celebrates the Last Supper, in which bread and wine are consecrated and then eaten. In some Christian denominations, children aged between seven and thirteen perform their First Communion, which is the first time they receive the symbolic bread (nowadays a wafer is used) and wine (now only given out on certain occasions). It is a very special rite performed by young Christians every year, and it marks their entrance into the religion in a fuller manner.

- When a Christian comes of age, his or her faith is ratified through a process called *confirmation*. This is nowadays done at ages between sixteen and eighteen, although denominations do differ on the age and not all practice it.

- Through the sacrament of *Reconciliation*, *Penance,* or *Confession*, a person's sins are pardoned after revealing them to a priest. Catholics are the ones who mostly follow this rite in modern times. Protestants reject the absolution of sins by telling them to another person.

- The act of *marriage* is also a sacred sacrament for Christians. Catholics are only allowed to marry once, but other churches have more flexibility, like the Eastern Orthodox Churches, where some permit one divorce and a second marriage. Many Protestant denominations do allow divorce, especially in the cases of adultery or abandonment.

• The *anointing of the sick* is performed on ill or dying people, particularly the elderly. A priest normally reads from the scriptures, performs what is called "the laying on of hands," blessing the person by placing oil on their forehead and hands, recites the Lord's Prayer, and, when possible, administers Holy Communion. This is practiced by many Christian denominations to this day.

• Men entering the priesthood get access to a sacrament reserved only for them: the *holy order*. This sacrament is understood from diverse perspectives, depending on the church.

East and West Drift Apart

After this huge stretch of land that encompassed the Roman Empire started growing apart in the fourth century, both managed to keep strong groups of Christian people. However, it was inevitable that the sections would begin showing their differences.

In the beginning, Christians were not organized under a single structure but were rather scattered among several societies headed by different patriarchs and bishops, depending on the region.

It was after the Roman Empire's division that Christians experienced the development of two distinctly separate Churches with divergent leaders and canonical principles and traditions, especially in regions outside the reach of Rome. This city had aimed at establishing itself as a prime position of authority within Christianity. Its bishop—afterward named pope—would start having increased power over administrative matters, even more than his counterpart in Constantinople and other cities across the Roman Empire, or what was left of it at least.

While different Councils had brought together all these leaders in the third and fourth centuries, at this point in time, they unleashed theological disputes one after another. Constantinople proclaimed its own pope. Syrian Christians started forming their own separate

Church starting in the fifth century, which later become the Syriac Orthodox Patriarchate of Antioch. Christians in Armenia and Egypt also developed their own separate institutions, forming the Armenian Apostolic and the Coptic Orthodox Churches respectively. Many other similar examples proliferated all over Eastern Asian and African regions in which Christianity had set roots.

Another feature that established a cultural difference between both centers—with Rome on one side and Constantinople on the other— was the fact that the West adopted the Latin language for its Bible and doctrinal interpretations while the East continued with its tradition of having all of the religious scriptures in Greek. Latin eventually gained the upper hand, especially due to the fact that the writers who used this language to spread and interpret Christian teachings gained more prestige than many of their Greek-speaking counterparts.

Most of the European tongues, especially the so-called Romance languages (Spanish, Portuguese, Italian, and French, among others), are an evolution of the original dialects from different regions mixed together with Latin words and grammar. The Roman alphabet we use nowadays also has a Latin origin. All this eventually made an impact on having Latin and Latin-derived means of communication as the main system in the West to disseminate Christian ideas, much more so than the Eastern-oriented Greek.

Political circumstances also added to these increasing East-West divisions. While the Eastern Roman Empire lasted, Christianity stood as the main religion in all of its provinces, from the western Mediterranean territories to the Parthian Empire (modern Iran) and all the way to India.

This situation of dominance for Christians in the East would change after a few centuries. Multiple Christian communities did stay entrenched in different parts of the dismembered empire, all throughout Persia, Central Asia, Northern Africa, and beyond, but they now shared this huge stretch of land with multiple other beliefs, including Judaism, of course; the new Muslim religion after the seventh century, which took Christ as one of their accepted prophets, although he is not seen as the son of God; as well as Hinduism, Buddhism, and Taoism, among other traditional religions in diverse parts of Asia.

The remnants of the Roman Empire in Europe also strengthened the Christian faith across the European continent but in a more absolute way than it did in the East. It was eventually transformed into the dominant religion for over the next thousand years, and it still holds that position today.

A few centuries later, with the 1054 Schism, also called the Great Schism, the Eastern and Western Churches formally decided to separate, with the Roman pope and the Byzantine patriarch excommunicated each other. This deep estrangement between both Christian groups would remain until the twentieth century when tensions finally eased after the Second Vatican Council met between 1962 and 1965 and a series of dialogues were set up among both groups.

Chapter 4 – Christianity Spreads Throughout the World

The Western Roman Empire collapsed in 476 when Germanic King Odoacer deposed the Emperor Romulus Augustulus. Some mark this date as the beginning of the Middle Ages in Europe.

Rome had fallen, but Christianity had not. On the contrary, it would only be a matter of time before it continued spreading—slowly but surely—throughout every region in Europe, all the way to its western and northernmost domains.

What people called the "Roman Empire" back then was, in reality, the Eastern Roman Empire, which ultimately became the Byzantine Empire, with Constantinople (originally Byzantium, nowadays Istanbul) as its capital. It had undoubtedly nowhere near the extent it possessed before the Empire's breakup, but it still retained much of its grandeur and cultural relevance—definitely more so than its Western counterpart, which was by then being constantly raided by all sorts of tribes.

Some scholars, such as eighteenth-century historian Edward Gibbon, blame the rise of Christianity as the cause for the fall of the Roman Empire, although others point to the constant "barbaric" incursions coming in from the western and northern borders and also to the internal corruption entrenched within the Western Roman Empire's institutions.

Constantinople

The Eastern Roman Empire became a bastion for Roman cultural preservation, and they also maintained a deep religious stance on Christianity, which lasted all the way until the fifteenth century when Constantinople fell to the Turks.

Presided over by Emperor Justinian in the sixth century, the Eastern Roman Empire's struggle to regain its former Roman glory was largely unsuccessful. There were constant tensions between Constantinople's patriarch and the pope in Rome.

In 537, Justinian ordered the construction of the magnificent Hagia Sophia, the epitome of Byzantine architecture and the center of the Greek Orthodox Church until it was converted into a Muslim mosque in 1453. This massive building maintained its position as the largest church in the world until the Seville Cathedral in Spain was built in the sixteenth century. It is nowadays a secular building that houses a museum.

All around the eastern provinces of the remaining Roman Empire, the multiple denominations that had sprung up—Armenian, Greek, and Syriac Orthodox, as well as Roman, Armenian, and Chaldean Catholics, among others—made it impossible to obtain a centralized institution such as the one seen in the West under the Pope.

A series of missionary journeys continued to set out from Constantinople with an emphasis on the Far East and Africa. Some of these were very successful, and others failed after a few centuries.

With Muslim hegemony in the region after the sixteenth century, Christian communities noticed a period of diminished influence and ultimately saw the withdrawal of large communities which reestablished themselves in other areas where they could more easily express their religion. In the twenty-first century, there are only about two thousand active Christians remaining in modern-day Turkey, for example. Other countries also experienced a demise in their Christian communities, such as Iraq, Syria, and the Arab states of the Persian Gulf.

European "Barbarians" Convert

By the fifth century, the former Roman territories in Europe had been dominated by a series of "barbaric" rulers, and the popes needed to learn how to deal with this new reality. Part of the strategy was to convert these unruly and pagan tribes from the north. The answer to this dilemma was the proliferation of missionary efforts, where monks, priests, and ordinary Christians took it upon themselves to evangelize the multiple European tribes all across the continent, all the way up to Scandinavia and as far west as what is today Portugal. It was a basic adaptation of the original missions that in the first century had come from Palestine into the Mediterranean territories.

In his *History of Christian Missions*, British nineteenth-century historian George MacLear asserted that the medieval period "was fertile in noble and heroic men, who laid, always in self-denial and self-sacrifice, sometimes in martyrdom and blood, the foundations of many of the Churches of modern Europe."[xi]

One of the earliest, as well as one of the most spectacular conversions, was that of Clovis I, the king who was the first to unite the Frankish tribes into what would later become France. He had married a Burgundian princess who was Catholic named Clotilde, but Clovis was still not a believer himself until a magnificent turn of events made him change his mind.

During the Battle of Tolbiac against the Alemanni in 496, Clovis suffered heavy losses within his troops. Desperate, he turned to his wife's god and prayed for help. Sixth-century historian Gregory of Tours wrote about this chapter in the region's Christianization in his book *Historia Francorum* (*History of the Franks*). He stated that Clovis had pleaded with Jesus Christ, a God who he conceded "gives succor to those who are in danger, and victory to those accorded who hope in Thee," to grant him victory over his opponents and that if he managed to triumph, he would start believing and be baptized in his name. Tours recorded that Clovis' prayer included the following words: "I invoked my gods, and…they failed to help me…It is to you I cry now, I want to believe in you if only I may be saved from my opponents."

Clovis I finally won the Battle of Tolbiac and kept his promise. He converted himself and his three thousand surviving men to Arian Christianity (although he later in life was baptized into the Catholic faith), hence the beginning of a new religion for the entire French region.

Another early and very successful case of conversion was that of the Roman province of Britannia, present-day England, where Christianity arrived between the second and third centuries. The Celts in neighboring Hibernia—the Classical Latin name for Ireland—had also been converted very early on even though they were never conquered by the Romans.

When the Romans left this region in the early fifth century, Christianity persevered, especially in Ireland and western Britain, although their isolation kept them from having contact with the religious advances going on in the surviving Western Roman Empire. A mix of original Celtic traditions and the Christian faith formed what was then known as the Celtic Church.

Germanic pagan tribes—the Anglo-Saxons—invaded the British Isles after the Romans retreated and met with other local tribes, such as some from Northumbria, who had resisted conversion while under Roman rule. Even though the Anglo-Saxons destroyed many of the towns where Christians lived, these people still stood firm in their faith, despite these being very dark years for them.

The Celts in Ireland, who already had their own particular Christian views, received subsequent Roman Catholic evangelization efforts at the beginning of the fifth century, like that of Palladius, a bishop sent by the Roman pope. Saint Patrick might be the most well-known missionary to work in Ireland. Patrick arrived from England in 432, and his work on the island was so successful that he became a widely revered figure and is considered the patron saint of the Irish people.

Christian religious fervor set deep roots within the Celts in Ireland. "They formed an advanced outpost among the western nations," writes MacLear, "and when evangelized by Christian missionaries, became, in their turn, signally ardent and successful preachers of their newly adopted faith."

The Celts, in turn, sent missionaries to England in order to convert the Anglo-Saxons and other tribes to the Christian faith. There were also several missions that came from Rome which had a strong impact as well. In the late sixth century, a Roman Benedictine monk was sent by Pope Gregory I on an evangelization mission to Kent. This man, Saint Augustine of Canterbury, played an essential role in the conversion effort of the Anglo-Saxons by winning over the King of Kent, Æthelberht, to his cause.

It was only a matter of time before the Anglo-Saxons converted to Christianity, thanks to the conjunct effort between the Celtics and the Romans, even though some friction inevitably arose between both groups over the years.

By the seventh century, basically all of the people in Great Britain had converted to Christianity. The Roman system had finally prevailed over the Celtic version of the religion by this point as well.

The Christian faith was so strong within the Celtic people that from the sixth century on, waves of Irish missionaries started leaving for many other European regions, even as far away as the Slavic areas that form Russia today, in order to help evangelize those that had still not converted.

Charlemagne (c. 742–814) is a prominent figure for Christianity in Europe, and he is credited with ensuring the religion's survival in most of the continent after his decades-long quest to bring all of the Germanic tribes together. He was successful in converting them to Christianity, often with quite ruthless methods. His infamous motto "to convert the Saxons by the Word and the sword" sums up his intentions well enough.

Charlemagne managed to partially revive the old glory of the Roman Empire by uniting most of Western Europe, and he was even crowned Holy Roman Emperor by Pope Leo III in Rome.

After the ninth century, several missionary efforts started their advance into the Scandinavian and Baltic regions, which were still pagan. This evangelization was intermittent over the years. Many of the people in these countries only became nominally Christian, as they also expressed their own pagan customs in a parallel way.

The Danes became the first to agree to conversion after the baptism of King Harald Bluetooth around 960. By the beginning of the eleventh century, two Norwegian kings—both named Olaf—were main factors in the country's assimilation into Christianity. It is said that Olaf Trygvasson, who ruled from 995 to about the year 1000, was the first one to build a Christian church. King Olaf II Haraldsson, who reigned between 1016 and 1030, was posthumously canonized as Saint Olaf for his important role in converting the Norwegians. The Swedes, however, did not make the final step into Christianity until the twelfth century during the rule of King Sverker (c. 1130 to 1156).

The first evangelization efforts in the eastern Slavic areas, present-day Russia, Ukraine, and Belarus, came from the Eastern Church—that is, from Constantinople instead of Rome. This is the reason for this area's Orthodox structure, instead of being more Catholic or Protestant. Two Byzantine missionary brothers from Thessalonica (present-day Greece), Saints Cyril and Methodius, pioneered the great conversion efforts performed in this area during the ninth century. They are credited for the invention of the Glagolitic and Cyrillic alphabets, with which they were able to translate and write the Bible in the original Slavic languages—what are now the Russian, Ukrainian, and Belarusian tongues.

Cyril and Methodius, who are also known as "the apostles of the Slavs," exerted a wide influence on the cultural development of this area. They earned universal acclaim for their work and are now recognized as saints by all three branches of Christianity—Catholic, Protestant, and Orthodox.

Christians vs. Muslims

Beyond the efforts to end pagan worship in Europe, Christians faced another challenge, this time coming from the east. A more recent religion—Islam—had taken hold in many Arabian tribes in the seventh century. They began a series of conquests soon thereafter, first starting with Asia Minor, taking major cities like Jerusalem and Caesarea. They also went on into northwest Africa, Egypt, Mesopotamia, Persia, and then Europe.

Frankish leader Charles Martel, Charlemagne's grandfather, managed to stop the Muslim invaders from the Umayyad Caliphate at the Battle of Tours in 732. This major campaign to conquer Gaul, what is now modern France, was led by Abd-al-Rahman al-Ghafiqi, the Umayyad governor of Cordoba. Aquitaine, located more to the south, had already been conquered by him. However, Martel prevailed in the end; Al-Rahman was killed in the battle, and this group of Muslims decided to retreat into Spain, never attempting an invasion again.

The Battle of Tours was a definitive moment for Europe, as Charles Martel managed to put a stop to the Umayyads' advancement. Yet some areas in eastern and southwestern Europe were not that successful.

The Umayyads took advantage of the weak Visigothic Kingdom reigning over Iberia, which prompted a swift and victorious raid at the beginning of the eighth century. Starting in 711, it only took eight years for Ṭāriq ibn Ziyād to conquer most of the peninsula after crossing the Strait of Gibraltar from northern Africa.

The Umayyads established a caliphate over much of Hispania (Spain) and part of present-day Portugal in what would be known as al-Andalus. Only a few regions in the northernmost part of the Iberian Peninsula were never ruled by the Umayyad Muslims, like the Kingdom of Asturias. During those times, Christians, Muslims, and Jews lived together in a coexistence that would alternate between peaceful and tense for the next seven hundred years.

It was not until 1492 that Catholic monarchs Queen Isabella I of Castile and King Ferdinand II of Aragon united the Iberian Peninsula into one kingdom, forcing Muslims and Jews to convert to Christianity or face expulsion from the territory.

After this date, Christianity was firmly established in all of Europe, with the pope presiding over all aspects related to the institution of the Church from his seat in Rome. Yet not everything was rosy within this large spiritual domain. Small frictions among some communities eventually created giant tidal waves that would fracture the Catholic Church's eminence over the entire continent from the sixteenth century onward.

The Crusades

After the seventh century, European Christians were horrified to see that much of what they called the Holy Land—an area located between the Jordan River and the Mediterranean Sea where Jesus Christ was born and started his ministry—was now dominated by Muslims. Many of those lands had been a part of the Byzantine Empire, but after several battles, they had lost them.

The situation was so desperate that Byzantine Emperor Alexius I asked the West for help against this "Turkish" threat, one of the strongest tribes back then which had converted to the Muslim faith.

Pope Urban II set it upon himself to organize a quest in order to regain those territories and put them back under Christian rule. The Church had much political and moral power during this period, so many people from all over Europe enthusiastically answered his call.

It was in the year 1095 when the first group of ardent Christians coming from different parts of the continent got together and set out east on their first "Crusade," as this quest would be called. A quite heterogeneous multitude joined in—knights, ordinary men, women, and even children—yet the trip proved to be long and treacherous, and many died on the way.

Four main armies arrived in Constantinople to join forces with Alexius' soldiers. Together, they conquered important cities such as Antioch, Tripoli, Nicaea, and, the "jewel of the crown," Jerusalem. After four years, many of the Crusaders returned home to Europe, although others stayed in order to attain some kind of uniformity within the conquered territories.

During these years, many Europeans started organizing pilgrimage trips to the Holy Land, but they were often robbed and killed along the dangerous journey. Thus, some groups of knights—often coming from profoundly devout religious orders—were founded to aid and protect these pilgrims, as well as pursue distinct military missions. Some of the most famous of these groups were the Knights Templars, the Teutonic Knights, and the Hospitallers.

It was not long before the Muslims embarked on their own crusade—the jihad or Holy War—in order to regain the territories they had lost. After 1130, they started recapturing ground, especially under the leadership of the legendary Muslim leader Salah al-Din[xii] (c. 1137 to 1193), known to Westerners as Saladin. This man, who became the sultan of Egypt, Yemen, Palestine, and Syria, managed to reconquer Jerusalem in 1187 from the Crusaders, as well as other cities in the region. He was famous for being a great warrior, but he was also generous, cultivated, and a person of great moral qualities.

The Europeans decided to start a second Crusade, which lasted between 1147 and 1149 and was mainly led by King Louis VII of France and King Conrad III of Germany. This second Crusade ended in a humiliating defeat for them—even Jerusalem was lost.

It was not long before Christians pledged to persist on their religious quest, and a third Crusade was organized, also called the Kings' Crusade. Between 1189 and 1192, one of the most famous kings of all ages, King Richard—called the Lionheart due to his bravery in battle—set off to face his nemesis, the well-reputed Saladin. Under his command, Jerusalem was briefly retaken from the Muslims, but both were military geniuses, so the fights were fierce.

Richard heard that his half-brother in England, John, was plotting to take his throne, so he decided to go back. In the end, a truce was made, and the Europeans returned home without regaining hold of Jerusalem.

A Fourth Crusade took place between 1202 and 1204 led by Pope Innocent III. The main idea was to recapture Jerusalem, but the Crusaders ended up sacking Constantinople, a city that Christian itself, in April 1204. This plunder of the city—which carried a great economic connotation, of course—paved the way for the Byzantine Empire's breakup.

The total number of Crusades is debatable, but there was at least a Fifth Crusade between 1217 and 1221 and a Sixth Crusade from 1228 to 1229. The last Crusade sanctioned by the Church occurred in 1291. Jerusalem was regained briefly in 1229, but the morale of the Crusaders was already quite low, and finally, the mythical period of the Crusades came to an end. The Holy Land stayed in Muslim hands for good.

The Far East

In the first centuries after Jesus' death, many missionary efforts were set up to spread his word toward the most eastward reaches of the known world. Several groups settled quite early in Persia (modern Iran), and they were at first met with persecution. Nevertheless, after 424, Christianity finally became established; however, it was with complete independence from the Churches in the west. Several local movements, such as the Nestorians (also known as the Church of the East) and the Jacobites, were founded with their own particular standards and were thus considered heretical by the main Churches. People who practiced these faiths were even banned from entering the Byzantine Empire. These groups of Christians performed multiple missions into Central Asia and beyond.

By the fifth and sixth centuries, the Nestorians were already established in India and China. The Persian bishop A-lo-pen reached China's capital, Chang'an—nowadays Xi'an—in the year 635. He was quite successful in spreading the Christian faith throughout the empire, founding monasteries and translating Christian texts into the dominant language of the time. Christian principles were encouraged to compete with Buddhist concepts. However, by the end of the Tang Dynasty in the tenth century, practically all vestiges of the Nestorian community had disappeared from China. Small pockets of Nestorian Christianity would remain present, but it was greatly diminished.

It would not be until the thirteenth century that Catholics would start their own missionary journeys toward the Far East—not only to China but also Central and Southeast Asia. Mongolian tribes had expanded westward, practically to the edge of Europe, and sought contact with the pope, whom they saw as the foremost European leader.

The Mongols, who were rather inclined toward Christian views, dominated over China during that era and invited the Church to send teachers and priests to the region. By 1289, the first Roman Catholic missionary, a Franciscan called John of Monte Corvino, had already arrived in China's capital. He was quite successful, translating the New Testament and the Epistles into the Mongol tongue and building a church. In less than fifteen years, he had already gathered a strong group of six thousand Chinese Catholics under his wing.

This positive outlook for Christians in China would not last very long, though. The Mongols were overthrown by the Ming Dynasty in 1368, and Christianity was no longer tolerated after that. By 1369, all Christians—whether Catholic or Nestorian—had been expelled.

Christianity would slowly start returning to East Asia after the sixteenth century, particularly with Jesuit missions. There were active journeys into China, Malaysia (where Portuguese missionaries were already present in the mid-1500s), Thailand, and Japan (where they ultimately failed), among other nations. Catholicism also consolidated itself very well in the Philippines. Multiple orders were established when the Spanish introduced the religion under the leadership of Miguel López de Legazpi in 1565, and the religion flourished. Augustinians, Jesuits, Carmelites, Franciscans, and Dominicans, among others, established convents, schools, and universities all over the country. The task was completely successful—almost ninety percent of the Philippines' present-day population is Catholic.

A Whole New World

The newly installed kingdom of Spain at the end of the fifteenth century was, of course, deeply Catholic (remember the expelled Jews and Muslims) and increasingly powerful. They were in a constant struggle with neighboring kingdoms over who would have the better trade routes and thus more access to the "riches" from the East, such as spices, silks, and minerals. These products were highly coveted in Europe yet very hard to get a hold of. Merchants needed to make long, complicated, and hazardous journeys in order to take these commodities from one part of the world to the other.

One man, Christopher Columbus, made Spain's rulers Isabella and Ferdinand a bold proposition: to look for a way into the East by going the other way, thus providing a novel route to those lands where the coveted products came from. He thought that by crossing the ocean that supposedly separated India from the European continent that he would be able to arrive directly at India's coast. How wrong he was—and how much the world would change as a result of this miscalculation. The rest is history. Columbus, an experienced navigator, did get to another shore after setting three ships, the Pinta, the Niña, and the Santa María, out into the sea. Yet he did not reach India; instead, it was an immense stretch of land no one in the known world had heard about until then (although Leif Eriksson had discovered it about five hundred years before, no one at the time knew this). A few years later, it would be called America.

Columbus died without knowing that the exotic lands he visited on his three journeys were a part of a different continent than India, which is why he kept saying that he had been in the "Indies" and had dealt with "Indians." But the Kingdom of Spain was presented with the most spectacular opportunity of their lives: a region filled with gold, silver, and other unimaginable treasures. And everything was theirs to explore, conquer, and eventually convert.

The fact that Spain and Portugal—two devout Catholic kingdoms— took control over all of Central and South America, as well as practically the entire southern territories of North America, changed the religious structure of these lands forever. It was an epic task, yet with a combination of persuasion and violence and with the construction of mighty institutions, the region's Catholic destiny would be defined for the next four hundred years.

The indigenous inhabitants first met priests and monks with a mixture of distrust and naiveté but also at times with outright hostility. Thousands of missionaries started leaving Spain for the daunting task of converting millions of these so-called Indians. There are estimates that Mexico already had over eight hundred priests already working in Mexico thirty-five years after the fall of the Aztec Empire.

After the nineteenth century, the American provinces gained their independence, but Catholicism remained with a strong foothold of millions of believers.

The process of evangelization in the northernmost areas of the continent was completely different, and this is due to those mentioned frictions among European Christians starting at the end of the fourteenth century and which led to a major schism less than one hundred years later.

Chapter 5 – Radical changes Within the Church

One thousand years after Christianity became the official religion of the Roman Empire, almost all of the European inhabitants had adapted to a unified structure in which religion completely dominated over practically every aspect of their lives.

The dogmatic power of the Catholic Church was firmly established in the region—perhaps too much so. This incredible amount of power eventually led to corruption, both spiritual and doctrinal. The Catholic Church had grown immensely rich. Some estimates indicate that by 1502, seventy-five percent of all the wealth in France belonged to it. The 1522 Diet of Nuremberg stated that fifty percent of Germany's wealth was in the hands of the Church. The decadence had reached all spheres, and it was even common for priests to grant women absolution to their sins in exchange for sex.

Feudalism also spurred the Church into a state of increased corruption during the Middle Ages, as many of the extensive lands under its control were not used for spiritual causes but rather for secular activities. This allowed for the sale of influences in which a "client" could offer a more lucrative contract for the use of those lands.

Many of the Church's decrees back then were increasingly divorced from what the original scriptures said. One particular issue—the sale of indulgences—had put many people at odds with ecclesiastical leaders.

Priests granted forgiveness through sacramental confession, but this was independent of the punishment one could receive for certain wrongdoings. So, the Church could give out an indulgence in order for people to make amends for those sins. Originally, people were required to undergo some sort of spiritual work, like visiting a sacred place or performing charity of some kind. Yet some people simply wanted to forego the need to perform these "punishments" and instead make a payment of some sort.

By the late Middle Ages, the sale of indulgences had become a common practice with the money that was being collected going toward maintaining a luxurious way of life for many within the clergy. There was, of course, a lot of disgust over this decadent practice. "The point of inflection," comments historian Peter Watson, "is reached in 1476, when Pope Sixtus IV declares that indulgences could also be conceded to 'the souls who suffered in the purgatory.' This 'celestial fraud,' how William Manchester[xiii] describes it, was an immediate success: in order to aid their dead relatives, peasants were capable of making their families go hungry."[xiv]

The leadership of the pope as a spiritual institution was also weakened in the Late Middle Ages. By 1305, King Philip I of France had wielded his influences to have Clement I, a Frenchman and personal friend of his, elected pope. Not happy with this, he then decided to have the papal court moved to the French city of Avignon in 1309, and it stayed there until 1377. After the court returned to Rome, a period known as the Western Schism brought about a battle to rightfully claim the papacy position. There were a series of popes and anti-popes being proclaimed and then removed one after the other. All of this weakened the papal institution among Europeans, who believed this to be a position that should not be tainted with normal political struggles.

The Reformation: A German Monk Sparks Change

An educated Augustinian priest, who was a professor of moral theology at the University of Wittenberg in Germany, emerged from obscurity in the year 1517 in a rather dramatic fashion. This man of deep faith called Martin Luther (1483–1546) nailed an academic paper of his authorship—his *Disputation on the Power of Indulgences*, commonly known as the *Ninety-five Theses*—to the door of the Wittenberg Castle, sparking the movement called the Reformation. It was a bold act of defiance against the Catholic Church, as this paper contained a series of proposals and concerns regarding several dogmatic and practical religious issues. Anyone who dared to defy the Church back then risked harassment, persecution, and even excommunication.

One recent revolutionary advancement made all the difference in what was to happen afterward: the printing press. Some eighty years beforehand, another German, Johannes Gutenberg, had made an extraordinary innovation to a machine the Chinese had been using for centuries in order to print documents in a serial way. This innovation was the movable type, which meant that letters could be adjusted according to the text that was to be reproduced and not a fixed block like the Chinese version. This enabled a faster—and cheaper—way to reproduce all kinds of texts.

Before the mass press industry started printing thousands of books, mainly the Bible, including the time shortly after Gutenberg's prototype came to life, reading and owning books were a privilege reserved for very few people. First of all, there was still widespread illiteracy among Europeans, and secondly, handwritten texts were very expensive—only the wealthiest elites could afford them. Monks were the ones in charge of the laborious task of copying manuscripts by hand before the printing press was revolutionized. The process to finish one book could take weeks, and the training these scribes went through in order to be able to reproduce letters and images was grueling.

The Church was also very adamant about not letting the common people get a hold of these valuable documents. They reserved knowledge for themselves, and monasteries were quite possessive of the texts they owned. Education was power, and those who had the educational tools—books—were able to exert that power in a more complete way.

The world radically changed thanks to the printing press, as it became an essential tool for education. More people were able to have cheaper access to books and thus more power at the reach of their hands and heads. So, when Martin Luther posted his theses, printed copies were quickly distributed throughout the region and beyond. This meant that thousands of people learned of Luther's ideas rather quickly.

In the beginning, Luther's idea was to present the Catholic Church with several considerations, not to simply go against it. But authorities were not amused at all by his "propositions," and in 1521, the Diet of Worms excommunicated him and condemned him as an outlaw. Yet Luther had his adherents, and under the protection of some German princes, he continued working and even translated the Bible to German—something that was unheard of since European religious writings were only read and written in Latin. This was precisely another key factor that kept the common people from accessing these works; it was impossible for them to fully understand the scriptures since very few could actually understand Latin. Luther firmly believed that the Bible should be taught so everyone could understand its message, and his translation of the Bible only increased his popularity.

Another revolutionary idea Luther promoted was that priests should be able to be wed. He did, in fact, get married to a former nun, and he bore six children with her throughout a long and stable relationship.

In 1524, a revolt of Germany's peasants led to the implementation of Luther's principles within the region. Lutheranism was installed as an official religion shortly after that in all of Germany, Scandinavia, and parts of the Baltic region.

Other "Rebels" Follow Suit

Luther's ideas spread like wildfire across many European regions, and shortly afterward, other leaders followed suit in adopting some of his principles.

By 1519, the sermons of a Swiss pastor named Ulrich Zwingli were making an impact in the city of Zürich, thus starting the Swiss Reformation.

France had also been hit with Reformation ideas by 1541. A French Protestant, John Calvin (1509–1564), had been exiled to Switzerland, feverishly working on several ideas for an innovative religious doctrine. He wrote his *Institutes of the Christian Religion* in Geneva, which successfully spread to the Netherlands, Scotland, France, and Transylvania. What became known as Calvinism was finally adopted as a formal Protestant Christian branch in many of these areas soon after.

The Reformation in England was implemented for a number of reasons which did not have much to do with religion and doctrine itself but rather with politics.

King Henry VIII was looking for a male heir, but his wife, Catherine of Aragon, had not been able to give him one. Of the six children they had together, only one—a girl named Mary—survived into adulthood. So, he asked for an annulment to his marriage, which Pope Clement VII denied. Henry did not waste time discussing this issue with Rome, and in 1534, he decided that he alone was to be the head of a new church for England.

Henry adopted a form of Protestantism imbued with many Calvinist ideas and finally got his way. He annulled his marriage to Catherine.

Yet the struggle to produce a son found many obstacles in the way, and Henry went on to marry five more times.

In the end, everything Henry VIII did in order to produce a long-lasting male heir was to no avail. His much-wanted surviving son, Edward VI, only ruled for six years, from ages nine to fifteen, before he died from consumption (what tuberculosis was called back then).

It is ironic that Henry VIII's two surviving daughters would be the ones to become the next rulers of England for many years after his death.

First came Mary Tudor—Henry's daughter with Catherine of Aragon—who for a limited amount of time tried to restore Roman Catholicism back to England. Her mother had been a staunch Spanish Catholic, so her loyalty lay with the pope in Rome. She was successful for a while, although only through the use of bloody methods in order to maintain religious discipline. Queen Mary ordered multiple executions of those who opposed the restoration of Catholicism, and these cruel procedures earned her the nickname "Bloody Mary."

After Mary's premature death due to illness within five years of her reign, her younger half-sister succeeded her. This young red-haired woman would go on to become one of the most famous queens of all time, Elizabeth I, and she ruled England for more than forty years. She restored Protestantism to the country, yet in order to please as many people as possible, she implemented the idea to go half-way, which evolved into the novel Church of England or Anglican Church, which took elements from both Calvinism as well as Catholicism.

The Counter-Reformation: The Catholic Church Reacts

The religious innovations that Luther, Calvin, and others had injected into many of the countries in northern Europe were met with slow response on behalf of the Catholic authorities. There were some positive changes due to the realization that Protestantism had come from a good reason, yet other outcomes stepped more into a darker side.

The Council of Trent, which met several times between 1545 and 1563, condemned the Reformation, although it did some deep reflection on the causes that had led to it. Authorities decided to keep many of the practices that had caused the anger of the Reformers but forbade any kind of abuses stemming from them. A set of new rules regarding the sale of indulgences and moral standards within convents, among other issues, were set up.

This new period of Catholicism after the Reformation is known as the Counter-Reformation, or the Catholic Revival. There was a shift toward more spirituality and better education standards. New religious orders were established, such as the Jesuits, which had a strong commitment in terms of intellectual achievements and rigid moral rules.

So, the Counter-Reformation was a period with higher levels of mysticism and austerity, but it also imposed strict measures that went to such extremes that it brought around the darkest episode of the Inquisition.

The institution of the Inquisition had existed since the twelfth century, mainly in France, Germany, and northern Italy, and it was dedicated to the fight against heresy. Some of their most infamous cases in those times were the torture and execution of thousands of Knights Templars, mainly for political and monetary reasons, as well as the trial and execution of Joan of Arc, the fifteenth-century French heroine of the Hundred Years' War against the British.

The Church had a great fear of heretical activity, but it also became wary of any suspicious attitude that could resemble some kind of rebellious stances similar to what had happened during the Reformation. It was too risky; they would only continue to lose followers, power, and more of their ancient possessions if they allowed it to keep happening. Many of the Catholic Church's properties—including cathedrals, chapels, and monasteries—in the lands where Lutheranism and Calvinism had taken root were looted, destroyed, or confiscated.

The institution dedicated to persecuting those who committed heresy was given new grounds to also investigate religious dissent, so after the period of the Reformation, the Inquisition escalated to new levels of cruelty.

The Spanish Inquisition: Terror Regime

Before the Counter-Reformation even began, the Inquisition's offices had expanded into Spain and Portugal, doing so by the fifteenth century. The Spaniards, in particular, had a hard time dealing with *conversos*, those Muslims and Jews who had converted to Christianity more often out of sheer pressure, practicality, and fear than out of conviction. Rulers Ferdinand and Isabella believed the installment of an Inquisition office within their territory would aid in these "problems."

The Dominican friar who was put in charge of the Inquisition would later become a synonym of horror and barbaric zealotry—the nefarious Tomás de Torquemada. From his post as Inquisitor General, he unleashed terror among many. Torture became rampant, and about two thousand people were burned at the stake. Even Saint Ignatius of Loyola, the founder of the Jesuits and a famed theologian, was arrested twice after being suspected of heresy.

Complaints against Torquemada went up to Pope Alexander VI himself. He was so overcome by all the terrible stories that he immediately led an initiative to curb Torquemada's power. This was achieved in part with the appointment of four assistant inquisitors.

The Spanish Inquisition's reign of terror did not end with the death of Torquemada in 1498; instead, the institution was taken to North Africa and to the "New World," those territories now being called the Americas which were under Spanish rule.

An Inquisitions office was established in Mexico in 1570, which persecuted heretics and Protestants alike, as well as *Marranos*, those converted Jews who were also still practicing the Judaic customs. From there, the institution spread to the rest of the New World provinces.

The Inquisition in Spain and America was so harsh that Protestant groups decided against establishing their communities within these territories for good. The infamous institution was not abolished in these regions until the nineteenth century. The last person to be hanged under its rulings was a Spanish teacher in 1826, who was charged with heresy.

The Roman Inquisition: Backlash Against the Reformation

After the onset of Protestant Reformation in most of the northern European countries, Catholic authorities back in Rome were desperate to activate some kind of countermeasure. Their influence had diminished drastically in these regions, and they were also wary of any other activities that could be viewed as heretical. So, suspected witches, Jews who had not converted, sorcery, immorality, and sometimes even those who pursued ideas akin to Renaissance humanity could be charged and tried at Inquisition tribunals.

The Inquisition in Rome during this time was far less radical than its counterpart in Spain, and many of the cases ended more in the payment of fines, confiscation of property, or bureaucratic charges than people being burned at the stake or tortured to death. Yet it did open the door for many religious conflicts to enter, which would submerge the European continent into strife, cruel persecutions, and outright war for most of the sixteenth and seventeenth centuries. It also brought some terrible cases of injustice and outright backwardness, such as the 1633 trial against the famed physicist and astronomer Galileo Galilei, in which he was accused of heresy for stating that the Earth revolved around the Sun. He had to spend the rest of his days under house arrest.

The Thirty Years' War

The Holy Roman Empire still existed in the seventeenth century and comprised most of the territories in western, central, and southern Europe. The rise of national sentiment within many of the states it comprised, accompanied by the fact that some were still Catholic and others had already adhered to Protestantism, eventually led to increased tension within its borders.

Charles V, the Holy Roman emperor during the time of Martin Luther, was met with the fact that his domains had been divided between Catholics and Protestants. He battled the German princes throughout his reign, although not with much success. The Reformation had come to stay in most northern, western, and eastern European states, and this was simply something he would not be able to overcome.

The final transition into Protestantism in the rest of Europe was that of continuous scuffles, revolts, and wars as well. The list of confrontations is long and bloody, and many of the conflicts lasted for years on end with the terrible consequences they brought in terms of human lives, economic disaster, and political instability.

The Tudor conquest of Catholic Ireland between 1529 and 1603 led to a series of revolts and the Nine Years' War, also called Tyrone's Rebellion. France suffered a lengthy period of war between 1562 and 1598 that pitched Catholics against Huguenots (French Protestants of the Calvinist doctrine) and left over three million dead. The Dutch War of Independence (1568–1648) set the Netherlands, Luxembourg, and Belgium—which had adopted Protestantism—against the reigning Spanish Catholic king. This conflict lasted a whopping eighty years, which is why it is also known as the Eighty Years' War. There was also the Anabaptist Münster Rebellion (1534–1535) in Germany, the Danish/Norwegian Count's Feud (1534–1536), the Strasbourg Bishops' War (1592–1604) in the Holy Roman Empire, and the Bohemian Revolt (1618–

1620), among many other disputes. All of these eventually brought forth the most terrible conflict of all: The Thirty Years' War.

The Holy Roman Empire was divided upon Charles V's death, and his successors installed some kind of tolerance toward Protestants. There was a relative period of religious neutrality and peace at the end of the sixteenth and the beginning of the seventeenth century in this region of Europe. Yet all this would change with the King of Bohemia, Ferdinand II, who rose to the position of Holy Roman emperor in 1619.

A deep follower of Catholicism, Ferdinand II actively sought to restore compulsory Catholic rule over his domains but was met with defiance and resistance on behalf of the German princes.

Protestant Bohemians revolted against Ferdinand, deposing his representatives and appointing a Calvinist, Frederick V, as King of Bohemia. Ferdinand was quick to counteract, unleashing the start of a war that would last thirty years and decimate a high percentage of the population of the areas involved.

The southern Catholic states of the Holy Roman Empire formed the Catholic League and initially crushed the Protestant rebellion. A large number of German princes were executed along with many Protestant leaders.

Other Protestant nations swiftly reacted to the way Ferdinand was managing the situation and condemned the killings, expressing their full support to the rebels. This complicated the situation even more. What basically started as an internal conflict had now become a full-scale continental war. Spain, England, France, Sweden, Denmark, Hungary, many Italian states, and the Dutch Republic all got involved in the conflict.

Catholic Spain had recently lost its domains in the Netherlands and set out to recover them. The Dutch Republic—now fiercely Protestant—lashed back. The Bourbon French, even though still mainly Catholic, decided to side with the Dutch Protestants in order to counter the Spanish Habsburg dynasty, an influential house that had held the seat of power in the Holy Roman Empire since 1438.

Clashing armies and mercenary groups fought all throughout Europe, unleashing havoc everywhere they went. Mortality rates soared, the economy was crushed, and the continent's population went through famine as well as many other sorts of unimaginable hardships. For instance, the plague sprang up, unleashing its deadly force on the people.

In sum, Europe suffered terrible losses during these three decades of conflict, which only ended in 1648 with the war's main forces—the Holy Roman Empire, Sweden, and France—signing a group of treaties in what was to be known as the Peace of Westphalia.

There are estimates that the Thirty Years' War eliminated about forty percent of Germany's population, with one-third of its towns completely destroyed. Other countries also suffered many losses and high percentages of people relocating.

Europe's Structural Change

The centuries following the Reformation and the Counter-Reformation radically changed the face of Europe—not only in a religious aspect but also in its economic, intellectual, cultural, and political structure.

The consequences of the Thirty Years' War were catastrophic for many regions. Nevertheless, the continent eventually saw the beginning of a new era, bringing about a period of greater splendor. Universities became stronger and more informed, thanks in part to Protestantism's drive for literacy; the age of the Enlightenment sprang up, mostly due to increased secularism in everyday life; the arts flourished more than ever before; and capitalism set its engines in fast-forward motion, bringing a never-before-thought-of quality of life to European inhabitants.

One of the major consequences of the Thirty Years' War unequivocally came to be more religious freedom for most

Europeans. Many states, whether they became Protestant or remained mostly Catholic in the end, now accepted most of the religious minorities within their borders. Many intellectuals influenced by the ideas discussed during the Enlightenment distanced themselves from religious institutions (although not from religion itself). Christianity's origins, morals, and doctrine came under discussion, creating, on the one hand, a more secular society but also infusing religion with a more modern outlook on many of its ancient principles.

On the other hand, Protestantism ironically also sent many to adopt a more Orthodox and conservative opinion of religion, even more so than traditional Catholicism. Some of the new denominations—mostly of Calvinist origin—incorporated highly strict views of Christian principles.

North America: Religious Freedom Off to a Rocky Start

Not everything was rosy in England after the country declared its independence from Catholic rule and established its own Church. The bug of religious freedom—the choice to interpret scriptures and doctrine in varied ways—had spread among many groups, not only in this country but elsewhere in Europe as well. A variety of religious sub-groups started flourishing as a result.

One of these movements, the Puritans, began expressing a series of complaints toward the now-ruling Church of England which they saw as corrupt. Persecution against them started soon after, and a large number of Puritans fled to Holland, where the freedom to practice their faith would not be as infringed on. In 1620, they heard that a ship—the *Mayflower*—would soon set sail to an area of Virginia in America where the British Crown would allow these religious dissenters to become established. Hoping to find this much sought-after freedom, they joined another group of settlers, who would later be known as the Pilgrims, and set sail. After facing a storm in the middle of the ocean, the *Mayflower* was thrown off its course and ended up more to the north than it had intended. This adventurous group built the first permanent settlement in this area, Plymouth, Massachusetts, where there were very few Europeans at the time.

The Puritans decided this was definitely the land to settle in, and from this date until 1640, thousands of their fellow believers flocked to the neighboring areas on the northeastern coast of the British colony.

Diverse lines of other rebel Protestants—Baptists, Methodists, Presbyterians, Quakers, and Amish—also migrated to different regions of North America, mainly in the east. They shared this assorted religious panorama with the own Church of England, German-speaking Lutherans, and a small community of Jews, as well as Catholics and Huguenots more to the south. Many of the states that make up the present-day southern United States were still Spanish and French colonies back then.

Nevertheless, not everything was as promising as it seemed. Those Puritans seeking freedom to practice their beliefs peacefully ironically looked upon other Christian branches with contempt, and they started persecuting all those they saw as "impure" or "imperfect" followers of Christ. They established a sort of theocracy within the provinces they had control over. Even witches were killed, with one of the most famous cases being the Salem witch trials between 1692 and 1693, where over two hundred people were accused of witchcraft.

So, the beginnings of Christianity in North America were not as "free" or pacific as many would believe. The clashes between different Protestant sects, and of these with Catholics, often ended in violence.

Spanish Catholics also performed their own executions throughout the colonies they controlled in North America. Kenneth C. Davis describes how in what is now the state of Florida "the Spanish commander, Pedro Menéndez de Avilés, wrote to the Spanish King Philip II that he had 'hung all those we had found in [Fort Caroline] because…they were scattering the odious Lutheran doctrine in these Provinces.' When hundreds of survivors of a shipwrecked French fleet washed up on the beaches of Florida, they were put to the sword."[xv]

This hostility between one group and another basically persisted throughout the colonial era until the United States' achieved independence from Great Britain. Some discrimination based on religion still persisted at the beginning of the Republic, so the country's Founding Fathers stepped in.

While he was still governor of Virginia, Thomas Jefferson drafted a bill in 1777 aiming to guarantee legal equality among all religions, even for those not professing any—a wildly progressive decree for the time. His words, "but it does me no injury for my neighbor to say there are twenty gods or no God. It neither picks my pocket nor breaks my leg," were to become quite famous in the following years.

Future president James Madison, as the governor of Virginia, sent out a decree that would lay the foundation to this religion/state separation. It stated that "the Religion then of every man must be left to the conviction and conscience of every…man to exercise it as these may dictate. This right is in its nature an inalienable right." With regard to state support of a specific religion, he noted that "the same authority which can establish Christianity, in exclusion of all other Religions, may establish with the same ease any particular sect of Christians, in exclusion of all other Sects."

Madison's allegations set the foundation on which Thomas Jefferson based his 1786 Virginia Act for Establishing Religious Freedom. Madison commented with satisfaction that the law was "meant to comprehend, within the mantle of its protection, the Jew, the Gentile, the Christian and the Mahometan, the Hindoo and Infidel of every denomination."

The new country's Bill of Rights also helped to put religious strife to an end—at least legally—by separating church and state. Its First Amendment stated that Congress should "make no law respecting an establishment of religion, or prohibiting the free exercise thereof." The freedom to worship whatever religion one wanted had been formally established in the United States.

Anti-Catholic and anti-Jewish sentiment was still widespread in the U.S. during the nineteenth century and persisted up to the twentieth century, yet religious equality and freedom were completely sanctioned under the law. This allowed for the spread of many new denominations within the Protestant branch. These novel churches gradually expanded from east to west—and eventually to the south of the continent—from the nineteenth century on.

The Baptists (based on Calvinist principles) splintered into several groups and are now independent of each other. The Church of Jesus Christ of Latter-day Saints (Mormons) was founded in the U.S. in the 1820s and set a whole new set of principles of its own. The American followers of the Church of England merged into several new denominations, mostly dividing themselves between the Episcopalians and the United Methodists. Another rather controversial denomination, Jehovah's Witnesses, also known as the Watchtower Society, was also founded in the U.S. during the year 1879 in the city of Pittsburgh, Pennsylvania. More recently, the United Church of Christ, officially formed in 1957, brought together many historical Congregationalists and other denominations of Puritan tradition. And the list goes on and on.

Catholics in the United States gained new ground toward the end of the nineteenth century when millions of Europeans from Italy, Ireland, and other countries where Catholicism was still the dominant religion started a lengthy process of immigration into America. This Catholicization was further strengthened with the more recent masses coming in from Latin America, where Catholicism was set as the predominant faith since its days as part of the Spanish Empire.

Chapter 6 – Christianity Nowadays

The days in which Christians fought among themselves in fierce wars with thousands—if not millions—of dead and tortured victims are basically over. We are in what we might call "modern times" where there are no meaningful animosities between the different groups. However, new challenges are arising.

Nearly a third of the world population today is Christian—this means over 2.2 billion people from all ages in every area of the planet. Christianity remains split into three main branches, each one with its own customs and traditions, although all are united without any doubt in their following of Jesus Christ and the Bible as a sacred text.

The Roman Catholic Church gathers around fifty percent of the world's Christians, totaling approximately sixteen percent of the planet's population. They are united under the pope's leadership, who is based in the Vatican, an independent city-state enclaved within the Italian capital of Rome. Also called the Holy See, it is the world's smallest country, with an extension of only 0.44 square kilometers (.27 miles).

The second-largest branch of Christianity falls under the category of Protestants, which was derived from the great sixteenth-century schism started by Luther and Calvin, thus being in existence for over five hundred years. These comprise around thirty-seven percent of the world's Christian population—some eight hundred million souls.

Lutherans still form a large, highly-identifiable group and are based mainly in Germany but have churches all over the world, especially where descendants of this country have migrated. Calvinists have evolved into several denominations, basically identified as Reformed Christians or Protestants. The Huguenots remain a strong force among many French nationals and are nowadays united under the Evangelical Reformed Church of France.

As was seen in the segment on Christianity in the United States, the modern Protestant divisions are numerous, ranging from National Baptists, Southern Baptists, Pentecostals, and Methodists, to Presbyterians, Episcopalians, Evangelicals, and Seventh-Day Adventists. It could be said that there are as many interpretations of Jesus' teachings as there are categories of Protestant churches. Some are more similar in doctrine than others, but in general, they express as many nuances as there are denominations.

Last but not least, the Eastern Catholic Churches, or the Oriental Orthodox Churches, comprise about twelve percent of worldwide Christians. The biggest of these eastern groups—and the second largest of all Christian churches—is the Eastern Orthodox Church (officially called the Orthodox Catholic Church), with around 200 to 260 million members.

Each one of the churches based in the east is still led by its own theological head, depending on the country or region they are based in. For example, the Coptic Catholic Church has its patriarch; the Russian Orthodox Church also boasts its leader, ruling out of Moscow; and the Ecumenical Patriarchate of Constantinople is run by an independent archbishop. This list goes on and on and includes Maronites, Armenian Catholics, Ruthenian Greeks, and Ethiopian Catholics. Each has its own leaders and conventionalities. Nearly forty percent of Orthodox Christians live in Russia. There is another tiny proportion—about one percent—of Christians that do not belong to any of the three major branches.

Regional Outlook

The Pew Research Center's Forum on Religion & Public Life[xvi] reports that although "in 1910, about two-thirds of the world's Christians lived in Europe, where the bulk of Christians had been for a millennium," this share of the Christian world population has drastically changed since then. They are nowadays "so geographically widespread—so far-flung in fact—that no single continent or region can indisputably claim to be the center of global Christianity."[xvii]

There is, however, an ever-increasing population of Christians in areas where they were basically non-existent less than one hundred years ago, such as sub-Saharan Africa and the Asia-Pacific region. This has changed the dynamics of the Christian population and institutions.

Contrary to global tendencies, there are more Protestants—mostly Pentecostals and Evangelicals—than Catholics in the majority of these sub-Saharan African countries. We can find a few exceptions, though; for example, almost half of the entire population in Uganda is Catholic.

Anyhow, this region is mostly Christian—sixty-three percent in total, according to the Pew Research Center—and the rest is Muslim, a circumstance which has given rise to ongoing tensions. There have been a series of violent clashes between both religious groups in recent decades that ended in bloodshed on more than one occasion. The Pew Research Center's 2010 *Study of Islam and Christianity in Sub-Saharan Africa* reports that "in eight of the nineteen nations surveyed, at least three-in-ten people said that religious conflict was a 'very big' problem in their country."[xviii]

The high population growth in this area of Africa also poses a series of other challenges. Its Christian population is expected to double in size by the year 2050, which means it will have more than one billion believers at that point. It will comprise an important proportion of the entire world Christian community.

The rise of secular practices in many places where Christianity had otherwise been the main religion until recently is testing its healthy future—and even its survival—in these areas. Especially in Western Europe and some parts of the Americas, fewer people go to church, baptize their children, or follow certain traditional principles, like celibacy before marriage—this is particularly happening within the millennial age group. Divorce rates and couples living together without getting married are growing on a global scale. According to the Chicago-based *Christian Century* magazine, nine churches close every day across the United States.

What could be the reason for this phenomenon? According to studies on the subject, there are multiple approaches to understanding the causes for this diminished Christian predominance in Western civilizations. For instance, many of the social responsibilities normally reserved for the Church—like feeding the hungry—have been taken over by the state. Also, after both World Wars, where a high percentage of the population suffered or died, people turned to disbelieving in a higher power.

Historically, almost all of the traditional international missionary efforts were Catholic and came from Europe, yet these are now rapidly declining. Protestant missions are now taking their place, with most of their missionary journeys starting out of the United States.

The rise of technology and advanced knowledge in several scientific fields has also taken a toll on traditional religious beliefs. Although many scientists claim that modern findings have taken them closer to God, the strict rules and doctrine within many Christian Churches tend to be less followed in view of scientific explanations to many ancient riddles. With a style of life more inclined to liberty and economic prosperity, many institutional norms are generally followed in a looser way—if at all in some cases.

Another problem some Christian groups face is the drop in the fertility rate. Europe's particular case of a declining population is especially noteworthy since Christianity was the only predominant religion for many centuries in the continent. More recently, people who profess other religions have been steadily settling in the continent, and experience higher birth rates than the Europeans who were already living there. Estimates indicate that this situation will radically alter the European religious layout within a few decades.

Christianity, nonetheless, remains strong. However, many new followers are adapting their own particular local customs and traditional beliefs to their faith, thus creating a new era of Christianity with its own characteristics. Christians in Africa, for example, have not discarded some of the ancient traditions of their original religions. Many still believe in reincarnation, practice witchcraft, use religious healers, and/or make sacrifices to their ancestors.

In an era of steady gains in material wealth, technology, and skepticism toward life in general, Christianity has adapted. As with every important turn of events in human history, religion will probably readjust itself in order to accommodate the new generations. Church leadership within every denomination will surely continue changing both in style as well as in many fundamental issues. In the end, the need for spiritual response and moral reassurance will always be there, and Christianity will continue to compel believers to seek the answers to many everlasting questions.

Conclusion

The long, complex, cruel at times but ultimately beautiful history of the evolution of Christianity have filled thousands of pages written by all kinds of authors from many nationalities. There are hundreds of books interpreting each and every aspect of its doctrine, leaders, beliefs, and destiny. People could spend their entire lives reading about this religion and never reach the end of the pages written about it. This gives us an idea of how the study of Christianity should have a multifaceted approach.

History of Christianity: A Captivating Guide to its Most Crucial Moments presents only a short summary of Christianity's evolution and introduces some main concepts in order to explain how this religion started and evolved. It also mentions certain historical facts and circumstances as a way to place it within a wider context. Yet the ultimate goal is to entice readers into learning more about this saga, which has many passionate supporters as well as fierce detractors. Many of the leaders and ordinary people who have left their mark on the evolution of Christianity were not even mentioned, although this does not diminish their extraordinary achievements. The list is simply too long.

Just by reading the biographies of the official saints, one can discover outstanding chapters within the Christian world. Some of them are revered only by Catholic, Protestant, or Orthodox followers, yet some are so outstanding that they are venerated by every Christian denomination.

Let us take, for instance, the life and philosophical writings of thirteenth-century Italian friar Saint Thomas Aquinas or the epic saga of Saint George, the Cappadocian Greek martyr related to the famous legend of him slaying a dragon. The biographies of these Church leaders are magnificent and filled with all sorts of fascinating facts of their times and work within Christianity.

There are also awe-inspiring female saints with captivating stories. Saint Ursula was a brave virgin who made the difficult choice of dying, along with thousands of other female companions who were with her, before being abducted by a horde of Huns in the year 393 CE. Another saint, Angela de Merici, chose this poignant tale of Ursula in order to name her pioneering project of female education—something mostly unheard of in the sixteenth century— thus founding the forward-thinking Company of Saint Ursula in 1535. And what could be more fascinating than reading about a woman who became one of the most famous writers of her time, who even created poems of erotic content—and in sixteenth-century Spain of all places? This avant-garde saint is none other than Teresa of Ávila, also known as Saint Teresa of Jesus.

These are only a few of the many equally and even more fascinating examples of the richness of Christianity's history. We hope this book sparks our readers' curiosity to find out and read more about this impressive saga in human history.

Part 2: The Kings of Israel and Judah

A Captivating Guide to the Ancient Jewish Kingdom of David and Solomon, the Divided Monarchy, and the Assyrian and Babylonian Conquests of Samaria and Jerusalem

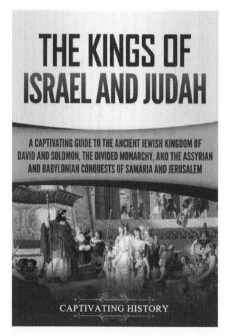

Introduction

The history of the ancient kingdoms of Israel and Judah and their kings is a story of epic heroes and villains. David was the God-chosen savior who fought giants, and the remarkable individual who inspired the world's greatest artists to create their immortal sculptures and paintings. Solomon is regarded as the author of many of the proverbs that we still use—and the ancient sources say he was married to seventy foreign princesses. The protagonists of this book also include famous rulers of the ancient world, such as Queen of Sheba and Nebuchadnezzar of Babylon.

You will learn how David unified the nation, but you'll also find out about his dark secret and its terrible consequences. You will discover all about the golden age of Solomon, the building of his Temple, and the legendary Ark of the Covenant—and you'll also learn how ruthless he was toward his subjects near the end of his reign. In addition to that, you will get to know the roots of the conflict between the Israelite tribes, why the Jewish kingdom had split in two, and how the two disunited kingdoms fell to the mighty empires of Egypt and Babylon.

There are two ways to understand the history of the ancient Israelites' kingdoms. We can either rely on the Bible or try to stick to undisputed archeological findings.

Here are the three top reasons why this book has chosen to follow the biblical version of history:

- Myths and legends (especially national myths of major kingdoms and empires, such as the foundation of Rome and David's triumph over Goliath) have always been a vital part of ancient history.
- Disputable or not, these stories have become the underlying foundation of the Western worldview, and as such, they still influence today's politics and tomorrow's history.
- They are far more interesting than dry facts. Archeological discoveries help us with chronology and data, but the Bible gives us all the substance.

Our knowledge of the prehistoric world often relies on legends. For instance, Homer (a shadowy figure himself) is our primary source of information on the Greek invasion of Troy. Likewise, the account of the Jewish people at the end of the second and the beginning of the first millennium BCE is not backed by much archeological proof. If we want to get to know these people, their motives and concerns, we have to rely on the stories that originated from their own oral tradition, were written down centuries later by the Deuteronomists, and preserved in the Old Testament and the Jewish Bible.[xix]

This book covers a timespan of about half a millennium. The first couple of chapters, which cover Israel's shift from tribal government to a centralized monarchy, tell the stories of the people and events initially described in the two Books of Samuel (Sam. 1 and 2). The rest of the book follows the storyline of the two Books of Kings (Kings 1 and 2).

Whenever it is possible, the events are explained from today's perspective, apart from any religious context, and with the awareness of some newer archaeological findings. However, since religion played a central part in the lives of ancient Israelites, the legitimacy of their kings was related to their special, often personal, relationship with God (in fact, all events, decisions, causes, and consequences in the biblical narrative are explained from that point).

Regardless of this difference in the availability and the quality of sources we have for different periods, the intention of this book is to offer you a clear, easy-to-follow narrative, and comprise all the most interesting facts and stories about this legendary world and its protagonists.

Chapter 1 – The Last Judges

It had been a while since Jacob (Israel)[xx] and his sons left Canaan (around 17-16th century BCE), only to end up in slavery in Egypt. Much later, in the 13th century, their descendants, led by Moses and Joshua, returned to the Promised Land, or as they called it, Canaan.[xxi] The twelve Hebrew tribes settled there and renamed the land Israel.[xxii] However, those tribes were not united, and they needed a strong leader to bring them together.

Up until this point, the individuals who had a supreme influence on the people of Israel and made the most important decisions were the so-called judges. These people were military and religious leaders, priests, and prophets, not monarchs. Their authority was often recognized by more than one tribe, but it wasn't enough to unite them all.

The Jews had always lived in the unfriendly environment, and now they were surrounded by the Philistine city-states and other equally hostile kingdoms. The disjointed tribes were incapable of resisting such forces. Israeli people needed a king to lead them to victory.

Samuel and the Priests

The man who, according to the Israelites' records, had the authority to identify the future king was Israel's last judge, Samuel. Both a military leader and God's prophet, Samuel was a tremendously important figure in Israel's religious and political life—just as important as the kings that he acknowledged, Saul and David.

Sacred texts of the three major religions—Judaism, Christianity, and Islam—recognize Samuel as one of the key prophets in history. His birth to a previously barren mother was described as a miracle, after which she devoted him to the service of God.

Samuel spent his youth in the tents of a priest named Eli, who was in charge of the sacred Tabernacle, and his sons, who also held priestly offices. However, these men were "wicked." Eli's sons had a habit of stealing and eating the sacrifices meant for God, and they had sex with various women at the Tabernacle entrance. Although disappointed by his son's actions, Eli kept them on in their positions and ate the stolen sacrifices as well. Then one night, God informed young Samuel that Eli's dynasty was doomed.

The Ark of the Covenant

The Tabernacle was a mobile sanctuary, a home to the most significant relic that, according to the Deuteronomists, had helped the Israelites win decisive battles such as the one at Jericho. This relic was the Ark of the Covenant, a wooden chest covered with gold, containing the two stone tablets of the Ten Commandments. This Ark was more than a relic; it was the symbol of God's presence among His people. In critical moments, the Israelites kept the Ark close and believed that it made them unbeatable in war.

Near the end of Eli's tenure as the custodian of the Tabernacle, Israel suffered a large defeat against the Philistines. The situation was serious; the Israelites had to do something fast. So they decided to bring the Ark of the Covenant into the next battle.[xxiii]

The Philistines were a bit shocked to hear that "A god has come into their camp!" Nevertheless, they beat the Israelites, sacked their camp, and seized the Ark. There's no doubt that they felt triumphant, but they were soon to encounter a not so nice surprise.

Eli was so disturbed by the news that he died. The wife of one of his sons died as well, due to premature labor. Her son was named Ichabod, meaning "No Glory." Without the Ark, and with its religious leader dead, Israel was broken.

Dagon, the Philistines, and the Ark

Philistia was not a centralized force. It consisted of five separate cities, and each of them had a king and their own main temple, dedicated to one of the Canaanite's gods.[xxiv] The most powerful Philistine city at the time was Ashdod (other cities were Ekron, Gaza, Gath, and Ashkelon). The Ark was taken there and put into the temple of Dagon, the Canaanite grain god.

The Philistines felt victorious. They had the Ark, and it meant their god Dagon beat the god of Israel. But the rejoicing did not last. The next morning, according to the Old Testament, Dagon's priest saw a disturbing image: Dagon's statue was lying facedown in front of the Ark. Confused, the Philistines returned the idol to its vertical position. It was even worse the next day. Dagon was not only lying down; his head and hands were broken and separated from the torso. The citizens of Ashdod were petrified by the Israelites' god's power, as that was the only way for them to explain what had just happened. In addition to Dagon's statue being broken, the people, tortured by tumors or hemorrhoids, felt the god's rage as well.[xxv]

Sick and frightened, the Ashdod citizens donated the Ark to the people of Gath, who eventually suffered the same destiny. The Gath citizens offered the Ark to their neighbors in Ekron, but they wisely refused the gift. The Philistines then placed the Israelites' relic on a cart drawn by two cows and sent it back to their owners.

Chapter 2 – Give Us a King

Eli and his sons were dead, so Samuel became the religious and political leader of Israel. He was also in charge of the Tabernacle, and he carried out all his duties marvelously for years. However, just like Eli's sons, his own sons became corrupt, and the people of Israel didn't want them to succeed Samuel. Rather, they expressed the desire to have a king and be just like all the other peoples.

Samuel disliked the idea of appointing a king because it meant rejecting God and himself as God's servant. However, according to the Bible, God advised him to "listen to the voice of the people."[xxvi] Before creating a major shift in the history of Israel, Samuel gave one last warning to the people. In essence, he said to the people that their sons would have to serve the royal army, their daughters would end up in the royal harem, and the others would be working on the king's construction projects. But the people didn't care about those warnings. They wanted to become a unified nation with a strong leader who would bring them victory over their enemies.

The Rise of King Saul

The First Book of Samuel (1 Sam.) offers two different accounts of how Saul was chosen to be Israel's first king. According to the first one, God tells Samuel that a young man will come and ask him something about his father's lost donkeys. The second variant says that the king has been chosen thanks to sacred dice.

Either way, people liked Saul. They were happy to have such a tall, handsome, and capable king.[xxvii] His reign started fantastic, as he crushed the majority of Israel's enemies. However, his triumph didn't last for long.

The Beginning of Saul's End

Very soon after the coronation, King Saul lost God's (or perhaps Samuel's) favor. There are, again, two stories about that. The first says that Saul didn't have the patience to wait for Samuel to offer a sacrifice to God after a battle, so he did it himself. The second story records that the king failed to follow God's (through Samuel) order. He was supposed to kill all of the Amalekites, but Saul spared the life of their king, Agog, and kept some cattle.

When Samuel approached, scolding the king, Saul started making up excuses and lied three times. First, he claimed that he had done everything that the Lord had demanded. Next, he said that the soldiers, not him, took the cattle. Finally, he declared that the livestock was kept for sacrifice. According to the Bible, Saul's disobedience ultimately made him lose the crown.[xxviii]

We cannot say for sure what really happened here, but this story tells us something crucial. The key difference between the people of Israel and the surrounding peoples was all about their religion and their ethics. For them, ritual acts, such as sacrifice, were not as important as right actions. Israel's prophets, including Samuel, kept repeating that following God's orders is all that matters.

Saul, however, tried to save his good name among his people and begged Samuel to honor him publicly—which he did, after he (Samuel) had killed the Amalekite king personally.

Chapter 3 – A Boy from Bethlehem

Saul was still a king, but God told Samuel that it was time to find a new one. The restless prophet followed God's instructions and went to a small village called Bethlehem. There he looked for a man named Jesse because God picked one of his sons to be the next king of Israel.

Samuel was impressed by the appearance of Jesse's eldest son, who was very tall, strong, and presentable, but God told him that it didn't matter how a person looks. This young man was not the one. Other sons were shown to Samuel, but none of them was recognized as the next king. It turned out there was one more son, the youngest one, who was watching the sheep. Samuel saw the boy and anointed him instantly. David was the chosen one. However, it didn't mean he's now the king.

Unfortunately, the only source about the life and reign of King David is the Bible. However, various archaeological findings, such as a fragmented inscription on the Tel Dan Stele which mentions the "House of David," tell us that a ruler named David did indeed exist.[xxix]

David's Lyre

David remained in Bethlehem, and Saul did not have the faintest idea what happened there. However, by an ironical twist, the king somehow meets the boy and decides to keep him close. Here's how it happened.

Saul had been tormented by "an evil spirit," unable to soothe himself. Seeking relief, he asked for a musician so that he could pacify the inner tormenter—and he is sent a wonderful one, a shepherd boy who played the lyre magnificently. The idea worked, and Saul appeared to be cured. Immensely grateful, the king promoted the boy and made him his armor-bearer. The boy, of course, was David.[xxx]

David's musical talents—along with God's will, according to the Old Testament—brought him from anonymity to fame. That's just the beginning, as the lyre was not his only weapon.

Slaying the Giant

David came back to Bethlehem, and his father sent him to check on his brothers, who were serving in the army of Israel. He arrived at the army camp and found something unbelievable going on.

In the middle of another battle with the Philistines, the fighting had stopped. The Philistines had offered to accept Israel's supremacy and become slaves under one tiny condition. They required someone from the Israelite army to fight and defeat their best warrior in a one-on-one battle.[xxxi]

The Philistine soldier was named Goliath, and he was between 6 feet, 9 inches (the Greek Old Testament) and 9 feet, 9 inches (the Hebrew Bible) tall.

At the moment of David's arrival in the Israelite camp, it had been forty days since Goliath started taunting and ridiculing Israel's army, their nation, and their God.

Saul had tried everything. He had even promised that he would award anyone enormously who dared to fight Goliath—with the result of a victory, of course. The guaranteed prize consisted of marriage with the king's daughter, wealth, and even a tax break. However, in forty days, no one showed the courage to encounter Goliath.

When David arrived, he was shocked that no one had the courage to stand up to this bully. To him, it was not a matter of physical strength; it had all to do with an individual's confidence in God. David was confident that God would help him, and he asked Saul if he could take this challenge. Saul admired the boy's resolution and offered him his royal armor (which would eventually belong to him anyway). But David was too tiny, and he couldn't carry the armor, so he decided to proceed without it.

David by Michelangelo (detail)[xxxii]

David was not completely unarmed. He had his sling—which he used numerous times to hold back predators and protect his father's sheep—and a few stones.

Goliath was puzzled and a bit offended by the sight of the boy approaching him with nothing but a sling. David promised to defy the giant in the name of the Lord, launched a stone with his sling, and hit the nemesis in the forehead. The giant lost consciousness, falling to the ground. David took the opportunity to grab Goliath's enormous sword and cut off his head.

The Philistines started running for their lives, and the Israelites chased them. David went to the Tabernacle and deposited Goliath's sword there as evidence that it was God who killed the giant. At this point, David probably did not know that he was going to use that sword someday again in the future.

Today, some theorists are trying to prove that Goliath had a medical condition known as acromegaly or gigantism which might lead to blindness; this might in some way account for the way that David was able to so handily defeat a giant warrior. However, the biblical account, our main source for information in this book, doesn't mention any possibility that the Philistine giant was disabled in any way.[xxxiii]

Chapter 4 – Saul Has a Rival

David became insanely popular with the people of Israel. As he started gaining many supporters, King Saul started to feel insecure. He was no longer willing to marry his daughter to David. In fact, he would rather see him dead. So, one day, having noticed that David was peacefully playing his lyre, the king threw his spear at the young man but failed to hit him. This was just the first of many of Saul's attempts to get rid of this charismatic teenager.

The next attempt was far more cunning. The king told David he could marry his daughter named Michal, but he needed to prove he deserved her first. The "bride price" that David was required to pay was one hundred Philistine foreskins. Saul apparently hoped that David was going to die trying to get these foreskins. However, the young man returned with two hundred foreskins, after which Saul had no choice but to allow David to marry Michal.

Saul wanted to kill David, but his attempts failed every time. David was not only very alert, but he was also everyone's favorite. Saul's own children, Michal and Jonatan, protected him and helped him evade a number of traps set by the king.

David, on the other hand, did not want to hurt Saul. On one occasion, he silently came very close to Saul and cut off a piece of his clothes, just to prove he could easily kill the king if he wanted.

He still respected Saul as God's chosen king, so he would not kill God's anointed.[xxxiv]

Saul said he regretted attempting to kill David, but he tried again several times. This time, however, he was more determined than ever. David and a number of men who joined him had to flee to escape being massacred. They went to the Tabernacle where the priests gave him food. David also took the sword of Goliath, which had been waiting for him. Saul found out about all this too late. Unable to kill David, who had already escaped, the king ordered his guards to kill the priests. No Israelite was willing to raise a hand on a priest, but an Edomite mercenary gladly obeyed. Only one priest, named Abiathar, managed to flee, and he joined David.

The Outlaw

Meanwhile, David managed to spare the king's life one more time, and Saul knew about it. After that, he again said that he forgave David, and even acted like they were still family (after all, David was married to the king's daughter). Regardless, Saul used every opportunity to try to murder his son-in-law. Even though he didn't banish David and his men, the king effectively put them out of the law and system. In order to survive, they had to do different things like charging the rich for protecting their flocks. One wealthy man called Nabal ("Fool") refused to pay, and David was determined to kill him, but the man's wife Abigail stopped him, explaining that her husband was a drunken fool. The fool eventually found out what happened and died of a seizure. David then married his clever and beautiful wife.[xxxv]

The future king was restless on the run. The Philistine territory was the only place where Saul couldn't kill David, so he and his men ended up living with the Philistines for more than a year, serving as mercenaries. It worked well for a while, but eventually, the Philistines started questioning David's loyalty.

David still managed to find a way to do the right thing in the toughest conditions. When the Philistine authorities sent him and his men to raid Israel, they went and sacked someplace else, then claiming that the war spoils were from Israel. The next such request was more complicated, as David was expected to really attack Israel during a massive joint attack. However, some of the Philistine kings didn't trust this Israelite and didn't want him to take part in this war, because he could suddenly change sides and become a dangerous threat. David was out of danger; the people of Israel and their leaders, however, were not.

Saul's End

The decisive battle was about to happen, and Saul wanted to know whether God would support him. Unfortunately, Samuel had just died, so Saul was forced to go to the ancient city of Endor to visit a medium, doing so in disguise because contacting the dead was forbidden. The medium summoned Samuel, who was not happy at being disturbed. The dead prophet told the king he would meet him and his sons the day after.

The next day, the Philistines devastated the Israelites in one of the bloodiest battles in the biblical world. Most of Saul's sons were killed, including the crown prince and David's dear friend Jonathan. The king had a deadly wound but remained alive. No one dared to kill him, so he fell on his sword to avoid being captured and tortured by the Philistines. In the end, the Philistines took his head and armor, and brought them to their god's temple.

Within a short period, the people of Israel lost all of their leaders—King Saul, his sons, and the last judge, Samuel. It was a critical moment in the history of this people. And now it all depended on what happened next.

Chapter 5 – King David

David grieved the deaths of Saul and, especially, Jonathan. His friendship with Jonathan meant more to him than the love of women, according to the ancient source.[xxxvi] However, David had to secure his place on the throne—and he needed to act fast.

Meanwhile, the tribes in the north (those that would form the separate Kingdom of Israel a couple of decades later, while the southern tribes would become the Kingdom of Judah) declared Ishbaal, or Ishbosheth, their king. Ishbaal was Saul's son, probably the last surviving one, although not the one whom Saul had in mind as the future leader of his people.

David Receives the Regalia

A man approached David bringing him the news of Saul's death and his royal insignia—the crown of Israel and Saul's amulet. This person hoped David would reward him for his "favors," which, he said, included killing deadly wounded King Saul, who begged for someone to put an end to his misery so he wouldn't be captured by the enemy.

David was not impressed. He was actually appalled by the man's bragging that he killed Saul. Killing a king of Israel, a "God's anointed" one, was a terrible crime, and David would not tolerate it. Instead of reward, the man received a death sentence.

Soon after that, a general named Abner, who had been serving under Ishbaal in the north, wanted to support David and change sides, taking a great share of Ishbaal's forces with him. However, General Joab, who had been serving under David, didn't trust Abner and killed him.

In this course of events, two soldiers arrived at the idea to kill Ishbaal in order to get rewarded by David. They slipped into Ishbaal's room at night, killed him, and brought his head to David. However, David disliked traitors—even those who betrayed his enemies. Just like the man who allegedly killed Saul, these two soldiers ended up executed for betrayal.

The King of United Israel and Judah

As a result of all this plotting, David became the king of the whole of Israel—both the northern tribes and Judah. Now, he had to make some important changes to the way the kingdom was organized. Saul's capital city was Hebron, in Judah. David chose another city for his base: Jerusalem. At this point, Jerusalem was a neutral choice. It was positioned between the north and Judah, and did not belong to any of the tribes' territory. By doing this, David managed to unite the tribes effectively.

He also had to unite the priesthood as well. Two different groups and their leaders, Abiathar and Zadok—one descending of Moses and the other of Aaron (Moses' brother and the high priest of Israel during the period of Exodus)[xxxvii]—made a claim to the position of high priest of Israel. To make everyone happy, David appointed both leaders as high priest.

Moving the Ark

Now that he had established the new capital, David wanted to move the sacred Tabernacle and the Ark of Covenant to Jerusalem.

Several anecdotes are linked with the transfer of the relic to Jerusalem. At least one man was struck dead during the procession because he reached out to the Ark.[xxxviii] The transfer was delayed and then resumed three months later. A new procession was organized, which included music, dance, and some nudity.

In Jerusalem, David danced before the Ark with his private parts exposed. The transfer was followed by a feast, and everyone was joyful—except for David's wife, Michal. She was not happy that her husband—and the king of Israel—uncovered himself in front of the crowd "as a vulgar man." However, David resented her criticism, and he rebuked her in return. Since she was so upset about her husband's nudity, he declared that he would never expose himself in front of her again. As a result, Michal remained childless.[xxxix]

According to the Old Testament, David wanted to build a temple to serve as the home of the Ark, but God did not.[xl] The king's hands were too bloody to build the sacred building. God wouldn't allow him to do it, but at the same time God was pleased with David's intentions and promised him his dynasty would last forever.

Chapter 6 - David's Downfall

David was at the peak of his power. He had just managed to achieve the unimaginable—to set up a truly unified kingdom under his leadership and to receive an eternal covenant from God. Moreover, he made Israel victorious by defeating so many of their long-time enemies. From such heights, one can go nowhere but down. And that's exactly what happens next with King David and, as we'll see in the next chapter, his family.

Springtime Temptation

Spring was the time when "kings go out to war."[xli] But David didn't feel like fighting, so he decided to stay in Jerusalem while his army, under the command of General Joab, fought the Ammonites.

The king was enjoying his leisure time and sometimes walked along the roof of his palace. During one such stroll, he set his eyes on an interesting sight: a lovely young woman having a ritual bath. David became instantly infatuated and sent his trusted men to find out who she was and to bring her to him. They did so, and after the first acquaintance with the king, the woman became pregnant.

The woman's identity made things additionally complicated. Her name was Bathsheba, and she was the wife of a Hittite named Uriah, one of Israel's most virtuous generals. He was on the battlefield now, fighting the enemies of David's kingdom—which meant that his wife's pregnancy might appear suspicious one day.

Concealing the Mistake

David had always been bright, so he concocted a cunning plan to conceal his wrongdoing so that no one got hurt. He called for Uriah the Hittite and asked him for a report on how the army was doing. Uriah gave him the report, and David seemed pleased. Instead of sending Uriah back to the front, the king told Uriah to go home and wash his feet—which is commonly interpreted as a euphemism for being intimate with his wife. But Uriah didn't do that. Instead, he spent the night sleeping on the steps of the palace.

The next day, Uriah explained to David that he just couldn't go home and enjoy his wife while the rest of the army was having a rough time in the field. It simply felt wrong to him (although it apparently didn't feel too wrong for David to remain in the palace or to sleep with Bathsheba; without even realizing what he was doing, Uriah criticized the king).

David did not give up. He gave a feast in the evening and got Uriah drunk. However, the soldier still wouldn't go home.

The king had a plan B, which was not as nice as the original plot. He sent Uriah back to the field and gave him a letter for Joab. In the letter, David told Joab to put Uriah on the front lines, so that he could be easily killed in battle. The plan worked; David married Bathsheba, and she gave birth to his son.[xlii]

The Punishment

One day, the prophet Nathan came to David to tell him about a huge injustice that had happened in his kingdom. A poor man had one lamb, and it was so precious to him that he treated it as if it were his daughter. There was also a rich man with many sheep. The rich man one day wanted to feed a visitor but rather than taking one of his countless sheep, he took the lamb that belonged to the poor man.

After hearing this story, King David got angry. The rich man's deed was outrageous, and he had to be punished. However, this story is a parable. The rich man is David himself, and he has stolen Uriah's only wife, whom he loved so much, to feed his "visitor." The king even killed the poor man to hide his sin. Nathan then delivered a message that, as he said, came directly from God. David would not be killed, and his dynasty would not be discontinued at this point, but he would still be punished in three ways. First, his family would be at war all the time and many of his descendants would be killed violently. Next, someone would publicly sleep with David's wives, because he secretly slept with his neighbor's wife. Finally, the child he had with Bathsheba was not going to live.

The punishments soon came true. The first son of Bathsheba and David died of an illness, and shortly after that, a whole series of unfortunate events started happening. It would be interesting to have another perspective on the events that supposedly took place on David's court. However, people—including the kings—were illiterate for the most part. The very few people who knew how to write were, in fact, the authors of the biblical books.

Chapter 7 – The Horrors

David was not the only man in his family who let his animal yearnings control his deeds, causing other people to suffer. This chapter is mostly about his sons, who did some equally horrible things and caused one of the most well-known family dramas in ancient history, in which more of David's children would die—including his firstborn, Amnon, and his favorite one, Absalom—this time by sword.

Amnon

Amnon was David's oldest son and the crown prince. At this time, he was dealing with an unrestrainable obsession. He was in love with his half-sister Tamar, and he couldn't control his desire any longer. Amnon spoke with his cousin Jonadab and told him about his yearning. Jonadab was entirely on his side and wanted to help him, and so he came up with a plan. Amnon would pretend to be ill and ask for Tamar to come and take care of him. The plan worked; as soon as Amnon was alone with Tamar, he raped her.[xliii]

Tamar cried from desperation, tore her robe, and put ashes on her head. Then she went and told her full-brother, Absalom, what happened. Absalom felt protective toward his sister and wanted to avenge her, but didn't pursue revenge yet. David was furious, but he wouldn't punish his firstborn son. It seems that the case was closed, but it was not.

Two years later, it had appeared that the whole thing had been forgotten. Absalom invited David to a sheep-shearing festival. Not surprisingly, David was not interested, so Absalom invited Amnon and the king's other sons. They all get drunk, and Absalom told his servants to kill Amnon—which was his plan from the beginning.

David's other sons fled home, where they mourned their brother's death. David was consoled that they were alive (he had heard that Absalom had killed them all, but now it was clear that it was an act of revenge). The king was worried about Absalom and wanted him to come home too, but the son was hiding from Israel. Two years later, he returned, asking for forgiveness from his father, which David granted.[xliv]

The Rebel

Absalom had returned to Israel for one reason—to become its king. And he would not be waiting around until his father died. As soon as he returned to Israel, Absalom started agitating, followed by his fifty men. He spoke to the people of Israel who traveled to see his father and ask for a judgment, and he was rather successful in winning them over.

About four years after his return to Israel, Absalom went to Hebron and declared himself the king of Israel. It is interesting and a bit ironical that he didn't go there in secret. Instead, Absalom had asked for his father's consent to go to Hebron, and he received it. Absalom had plenty of followers at this point, and people continued coming over to his side.

According to the biblical text, Absalom was stunningly handsome, with long, abundant hair. His appearance was impressive, and he was just the kind of leader the people of Israel wanted to have.

Moreover, he was cordial with people, kissed all of them, and promised to help them as soon as he became the king of Israel.[xlv] It is no wonder that many changed sides, including one of David's wisest counselors, Ahithophel.

David heard that Absalom had declared himself king in Hebron and he knew what came next—the crown pretender would come to capture Jerusalem with his army of supporters. Reluctant to fight with his own son, David summoned his army and much of the population and fled the capital. The only people who stayed in Jerusalem were ten concubines, whose responsibility was to look after the palace, the priests who looked after the Ark, and a man named Hushai, whom David had left behind to spy on Absalom.

"Absalom, my son, my son!"[xlvi]

Absalom arrived at Jerusalem, and since there's no one to fight against, he wondered what he could do next in order to make his victory more convincing. His (formerly his father's) counselor, Ahithophel, suggested that the new king should sleep with David's concubines and that he should do it in front of the people of Israel. So, he did exactly that—he slept with all the remaining concubines in a tent on the wide palace roof, and he did it in the middle of the day. That way, he conveniently fulfilled the prophecy—David's first son with Bathsheba had already died, Amnon was undone violently, and now someone had just slept with David's women in public.[xlvii]

In the end, though, David's men routed Absalom's in the forest of Ephraim, and Absalom was forced to escape. While he was fleeing riding a mule, his hair got entangled with some tree branches. The mule escaped without him, and he was left hanging until Joab found him. The general disobeyed David's instruction—the king wanted his son to remain unhurt—and had Absalom killed.

David was very upset by Absalom's death, and he lamented: "O my son Absalom, […] Would I had died instead of you."[xlviii]

Census and Plague

Several years later, David wanted to find out how many soldiers there were in his kingdom able and ready to fight in his army, so he decided to take a census of Israel. After nearly ten months, General Joab had the results—there were eight hundred thousand capable men in Israel and five hundred thousand in Judah.

However, these results were not final. Immediately after the census, a deadly disease struck David's kingdom, killing seventy thousand people in three days. According to the Bible, the pestilence comes as God's punishment for taking the census.[xlix] David is supposed to rely on God only, and not on the number of soldiers he could gather.

To end the plague, David bought a piece of land with a threshing floor, built an altar on the site, and offered a sacrifice—and this is exactly the spot where, years later, David's son, Solomon, would build the famous Temple of Jerusalem.

Chapter 8 – King Solomon

David was still the king of all of Israel, including Judah. Israel and Judah still represented the two groups of Jewish tribes inhabiting northern and southern territories of the kingdom. They were soon to become separate kingdoms, but right now, everything seemed to be in order.

However, the king was weak and also impotent. The First Book of Kings in the Old Testament says David is cold in his bed, and his servants and family do all they can to help him. They eventually bring him a lovely girl named Abishag to warm him up but to no avail. The king surely is less cold than before, but nothing happens further.[1]

In ancient Israel, the lack of potency was closely linked with the lack of any other power a king may have, and it suggested the end was near. And so happened the inevitable—the king's sons began strategizing around the succession.

As we've seen in the previous two chapters, three of the king's sons—the baby boy he had with Bathsheba, and then Amnon and Absalom—had already died. But the killing was not over. Even though David had allegedly promised Bathsheba that their other son,

Solomon, would succeed him, there were some other people who disagreed with that plan.

Solomon's Path to the Throne

David's successor, Solomon, would not just make his father's greatest idea come true by building the "house" for God. He was also to become Israel's most successful ruler and made his people one of the most affluent and influential nations in the world. But first he had to become the king, and it was not an easy task.

Things were a bit complicated at this point as Solomon was not David's eldest son who survived. Adonijah was older than Solomon, and he was ready to claim the right to the throne. He had some substantial followers as well. The long list of his supporters included one of the two high priests, Abiathar, as well as General Joab. Other influential figures, such as priest Zadok, prophet Nathan, and some of Israel's bravest warriors remained loyal to David, who was still alive when Adonijah crowned himself just outside the walls of Jerusalem.[li]

David immediately abdicated and declared Solomon the true king of Israel. The word spread and people started deserting Adonijah's forces. The throne pretender fled to God's altar and remained there until Solomon promised he wouldn't kill him—unless he tried to usurp the throne again.

David's Last Advice

David was about to die, and he called for his son and successor, Solomon, to give him some final advice. He told him to love and obey God so that his kingdom would thrive and his sons would remain on the throne of Israel forever.[lii]

In addition to that, David recommended Solomon to get rid of two particular men, whose activities might be dangerous in the near future. The first man was General Joab, who had served David for ages and was very brave and successful, but who also killed people who were under David's explicit protection more than once—and who just supported Adonijah against the rightful king of Israel. The second man was named Shimei, and he was currently supporting David but had cursed and betrayed him in the past, and thus could not be trusted.

David died, and Solomon did as instructed. He had the two men killed and, eventually, killed Adonijah too. Adonijah had tried to usurp the throne again, although in a subtler way: by marrying Abishag, David's last and youngest wife (who was apparently still a virgin).[liii] The former high priest, Abiathar, was not killed, but he was denounced and banished from Jerusalem.

The Legendary Wisdom of Solomon

Solomon had perhaps been born with a stellar mind, but the Bible says he was awarded it when he became the king.[liv] He followed David's advice, respected God, and lived and ruled rightfully—then one night, God approached him and said, "Ask what I should give you."[lv]

Solomon had the opportunity to choose between overwhelming power, longevity, wisdom, wealth, and other amazing rewards—and he chose wisdom. As he explained, he needed a wise mind to understand good and evil, and to rule his people justly.

God was happy with Solomon's choice.[lvi] In addition to epic wisdom, the king was awarded everything else: health, wealth, and power.

The next day, Solomon had the chance to demonstrate the wisdom he had just been given. In the ancient world, the king held the role of the supreme judge in all legal cases, and there stood a tricky case before him. Two prostitutes approached him with a newborn baby. The two women lived under one roof, and each of them had a baby recently. However, one baby died, while the other survived. Now both women claimed the surviving baby belonged to her. It was up to the king to decide who the real mother was—and there was absolutely no evidence to back any women's story. No problem at all; Solomon knew exactly how to identify the birth mother. He asked his servants for a sword and said he'll give each mother half of the baby. One of them did not object to the decision, but the other started crying and begging the king to give the baby to the other woman, just to keep the child unharmed. Solomon recognized the true mother's love and gave the child to her.

The Judgement of Solomon by Peter Paul Rubens (1617) [lvii]

Solomon's Glory and the Temple

Having secured his position on the throne, King Solomon worked on the strengthening of his kingdom. The walls and gates of all major cities were rebuilt, and the administration was established in several regional centers, which functioned well.

Solomon's household was magnificent. He was married to one thousand women, including hundreds of foreign princesses.[lviii] The king also took care of many horses and chariots that he owned by building impressive stables that also testified about the wealth of Israel.

In addition to that, Solomon constructed an impressive fleet and increased maritime trade on the Red Sea. But nothing was as impressive as his construction projects. His palace was built during a period of thirteen years. Just next to the palace, there was the Temple that hosted all the relics that used to reside in the Tabernacle.[lix]

The building of Solomon's Temple was particularly interesting. Construction had lasted for seven years, and Solomon had built it in a kind of partnership with King Hiram of Tyre, who provided the much-needed cedar lumber. But at the end, it was the people of Israel who paid for it and did all the work through forced labor.[lx]

The Decline

Solomon was at the peak of his power. He enjoyed enormous admiration from his subjects and especially other nations' rulers, and he maintained excellent relationships with most of them. The queen of Sheba visited him and testified about his breathtaking fortune. She had heard a lot about the splendor Solomon enjoyed and she didn't believe it, but once she saw it, she realized everything was even more magnificent than what her people described to her. (A later legend says King Solomon and the Queen of Sheba had a son together, but the Bible says nothing about it.) However, this state didn't last forever as even Solomon himself succumbed to temptations.

From the biblical point of view, Solomon's greatest mistake is that he started valuing the gods that his foreign wives respected, thus slowly abandoning Jewish monotheism. Things that started happening after his death—such as the split of the empire (see the next chapter) and the subsequent falls of both new empires are traditionally interpreted as the punishment for Solomon's later polytheism and his cherishing of pagan deities.

Another very palpable mistake that Solomon made is related to the way he governs the kingdom in his later years. Among the twelve tribes of Israel, he clearly gave special treatment to the tribe that he belonged to—Judah. Solomon had divided the kingdom into twelve administrative districts, but those did not correspond to the older tribal borders, but on some geographical features. Only the territory of Judah appeared to be intact, and that's not all. Each district needed to provide laborers to work on new building projects and to pay taxes. Again, Judah was spared. Not only did the people of Judah not have to pay taxes, but most of the money that had been gathered elsewhere ended up in this district, and it was used for their fortifications. On top of that, Solomon had sold some twenty cities that belonged to northern tribes to King Hiram.[lxi]

The Future Kings: Jeroboam and Rehoboam

Solomon noticed a son of one of his servants, a talented and hardworking young man named Jeroboam, and gave him a promotion. Jeroboam was in charge of some construction works in the capital. One day, a prophet approached him and told him he had been chosen to rule ten of the twelve tribes of Israel.

These ten tribes were eager to leave Solomon behind and follow the new leader. But the future king knew Solomon would want to kill him, so he fled to Egypt, where he stayed until the king's death. Solomon eventually died, and his son Rehoboam succeeded him on the throne of Israel.

Chapter 9 – Divided Monarchy

With Solomon's death, the golden age of prosperity that Israel enjoyed under the reign of David and Solomon had ended, along with any notion of the stability of the nation—together with. The tribes were at odds already, and now they were just a step away from parting ways forever. Where there was the great kingdom of Israel, two minor kingdoms appeared—Israel (consisting of the ten tribes in the northern part of the previous kingdom) and Judah.

The ages that followed were full of conflicts, both political and religious. About two centuries later, Israel would fall to the powerful Assyrian Empire. Another century and a half later, Judah would collapse as well, to another colossal force—the Babylonians, who would seize David's capital and ruin Solomon's Temple.

But in the meantime, there are dozens of kings of the two kingdoms whose lives and deeds, albeit often unheroic, deserve our attention.

Rehoboam – The Unwise Son of the Wise

The split-up of the kingdom may have been a consequence of the late Solomon's polytheism, but his unjust behavior toward the northern tribes contributed to the divide, and his successor had just added salt to the wound.

King Rehoboam visited the northern territories to make everyone was aware that he was the one in charge. He learned that people were unhappy with Solomon's taxation policy and forced labor, and that they wanted to know whether the new king would discontinue these policies.

Two groups of royal advisers offered conflicting advice to the king. The elder ones told him to be careful if he wanted the northern tribes to accept him, and to promise them whatever they wanted. The younger counselors disagreed—the king should show those rebellious crowds who's in charge. Rehoboam liked the latter advice and said a horrible thing to the people: "My father made your yoke heavy, but I will add to your yoke; my father beat you with whips, but I will beat you with scorpions!"[lxii] Rehoboam, of course, had no authority to force all those people to serve him, and they immediately declared independence.

From then on, the union of northern tribes would be called the Kingdom of Israel or, alternatively because they chose Samaria as their capital city, the Kingdom of Samaria. Rehoboam and his successors (David's dynasty) would rule the Kingdom of Judah from Jerusalem. Judah would stay relatively stable for a longer period, and its dynasty would last for more than 400 years (from David's crowning).

Jeroboam and the New Idols

Jeroboam (see chapter 8) was immediately accepted as the new king of an independent Israel, and he did his best to secure his position on the throne. Since religion played an enormous role in the life of the Israelites, the new king was afraid he would lose some of his subjects if they kept attending public religious festivals in Jerusalem. To prevent that, he built two new cult centers in the cities of Dan and Bethel and set up a golden bull (an ancient symbol of virility) at each site. Furthermore, he declared that those calves were the gods who really set the people of Israel free from slavery under Egyptians.[lxiii]

The biblical account says that Jeroboam and his successors are condemned because they abandoned God and embraced the deities that resemble Baal, the storm god worshiped by the Canaanites.

Shishak's Invasion and the Ark's Mysterious Disappearance

Meanwhile, in the south, the Egyptian Pharaoh Shishak used the chaos around the separation and attacked Judah, as well as a number of other cities; he gathered all the treasures from Jerusalem and then returned to the Nile Valley.[lxiv]

The biblical Shishak was actually the pharaoh named Sheshonq I. An inscription on his temple at Karnak says that he led a major campaign in the area today known as the Levant and that he crushed a number of cities. Yet, since most of the text is illegible, we can't be sure whether Jerusalem was actually on the list.[lxv]

No one knows what happened to the Ark of the Covenant. Maybe Shishak took it, or maybe it was hidden somewhere beneath the Temple. One story even involves the son of King Solomon and the Queen of Sheba.

Since the time of the Ark's puzzling disappearance from the biblical narrative, various researchers claimed they had a trace and knew where the Ark was located. Some sources claim the object is located in the Church of Our Lady Mary of Zion in Ethiopia, where it is kept under guard in a treasury.[lxvi] The Lemba people of South Africa and Zimbabwe claim they are in possession of the Ark.[lxvii] Various hypotheses say that the Ark is located either in the Chartres Cathedral in France, Tutankhamun's tomb in Egypt, the Basilica of St. John Lateran in Rome, or somewhere in the USA (where it was allegedly taken at the beginning of World War I. The quest for the missing Ark has gradually become a part of popular culture.

The Ark of the Covenant was not listed among the treasures that the Assyrian king Tiglath-pileser III took from Jerusalem.[lxviii] It has disappeared from the biblical narrative, and it's been gone ever since.

Chapter 10 – The Kings of the Divided Monarchy Until the Fall of Israel

We don't know much detail about the next couple of kings of Israel (and Judah). The old account says most of them failed to produce a lasting dynasty. Jeroboam's son, Nadab, ruled for only two years; he was killed (along with all of his male relatives) by a usurper, and the next king, named Baasha. Baasha reigned for 23 years, but his son, Elah, suffered the same destiny as Nadab—after two years of reign, he was assassinated by a military commander named Zimri, who in turn was killed by another commander. Zimri's reign was the shortest one in the history of Israel, as it only lasted seven days.

Omri, the commander who killed Zimri, became the king who managed to build a dynasty that lasted for a couple of generations (forty years in total), which included the next three kings: Ahab, Ahaziah, and Jehoram. The years during which these kings ruled Israel were full of conflicts and alliances (including an alliance with Judah) against aggressive neighbors. One example of an alliance with the neighboring tribes is the marriage of the crown prince,

Omri's eldest son, Ahab, with Jezebel, a Phoenician princess. Omri's military campaigns are among the first such actions that are documented by an undisputed historical source—the inscription on the Mesha Stele, also known as the Moabite Stone, says that Omri invaded Moab, but Moab later managed to suppress Omri's sons.[lxix]

Ahab, Jezebel, and the Prophet Elijah

Just like the great majority of Israel's kings after Jeroboam, King Ahab worshiped various deities, including the Canaanite god Baal and the goddess Asherah. But that was not his—and his wife's—greatest crime. Ahab and Jezebel cold-bloodedly committed a serious murder: they had an innocent man killed only to gain some of his possessions.[lxx]

A man named Naboth lived next to the king's palace, and he had a first-class vineyard. Ahab wanted to buy that vineyard from his neighbor, but Naboth wouldn't sell it. The king was upset, even to the point of losing his appetite, and eventually, his wife Jezebel came up with an idea. She paid two men to claim that they heard Naboth cursing God and Ahab. Cursing the king and God were major offenses (even though he worshiped a number of gods, Ahab still respected the God of the Israelites as well—apparently, he didn't find the two religions mutually exclusive), and Naboth was promptly executed.

Ahab obtained the vineyard, but soon after that, a prophet named Elijah approached him, telling him that both he and his wife would die for what they did to Naboth and that dogs would lick their blood. Soon after that, Elijah successfully (and rather miraculously) fought religious battles against the worshipers of Baal.[lxxi] Ahab ended up killed in a battle, thus fulfilling Elijah's prophecy.

Elijah was one of Israel's major prophets, and according to the Bible, he had three more tasks to accomplish. He needed to anoint the next kings of Israel and Aram (a neighboring state) and to appoint his disciple, Elisha, as his successor. Elijah completed the third assignment, then miraculously crossed the Jordan River where a heavenly chariot picked him up and took him away.[lxxii] The first two assignments were then left to Elisha. First of all, he needed to anoint Jehu as the new king of Israel.

A Transitory Truce: Ahaziah and Two Jorams

Meanwhile, the rulers and people of Israel and Judah were enjoying an unusually peaceful period. Judah's crown prince Jehoram (or Joram) had married Israel's late king Ahab's sister Athaliah. Their son, Ahaziah, was the next on the throne of Judah, and he continued a peaceful policy toward Israel. The new king of Israel was also named Joram. Joram's Israel and Ahaziah's Judah jointly fought the people of Aram.

Joram became wounded, and the two kings went to Jezreel together to recover. However, they both get killed in a violent uprising.[lxxiii]

Jehu

Jehu was the general in charge of Israel's army, and he was still on the battlefield while King Joram recovered at Jezreel. During one meeting with his officers, an unnamed prophet (allegedly sent by Elisha) approached him and anointed him, saying that he was chosen by God to punish Ahab's dynasty for the sins that the late king and Jezebel committed. The army supported Jehu, who then went to Jezreel.

When they heard Jehu was approaching the city, Joram and Ahaziah realized something bad was going to happen, but all the men they send away to find out Jehu's intentions promptly changed sides and never returned. The two kings remained all alone. Jehu arrived and killed Joram while explaining what he's doing. Ahaziah was mortally wounded as well.[lxxiv] Jezebel was killed, and most of her body was eaten by dogs. In addition to that, Jehu beheaded everyone who was related to Ahab either by blood or by any other way.

Everyone who had ever supported Ahab's dynasty died violently during this upheaval.

The next in line were the priests of Baal. Jehu gathered them all for a celebration and proposed that they have a sacrifice to Baal. The priests had no idea that it was them who were to be sacrificed, but that's exactly what happened next. Soldiers entered the temple of Baal, killed all the priests, and then completely destroyed the temple.[lxxv]

Jehu remained on the throne of Israel for twenty-eight years. His descendants ruled the kingdom for five generations, until the assassination of his great-great-grandson, Zechariah.

Athaliah and Joash of Judah

Meanwhile, in Judah, King Ahaziah's mother, Athaliah, found out her son was dead and decided she should rule Judah personally. To achieve that, she had all the male heirs to the throne killed. She didn't know, however, that the late king's sister named Jehosheba managed to hide one of her brothers—a baby named Joash—in the Temple. Seven years later, the High Priest Jehoiada declared Joash the king of Israel, and Athaliah was promptly killed.[lxxvi]

King Joash ruled in Judah for forty years, with the help of Priest Jehoiada. They used the donations collected at the Temple to repair the Temple. Other treasures were spent to bribe Hazael, the king of Aram, to not destroy the city of Jerusalem. Eventually, Joash was killed by his servants, Jozacar and Jehozabad. His son Amaziah succeeded him on the throne of Israel.

Chapter 11 – Ten Lost Tribes: The Destruction and Fall of Israel

Israel and Judah were in a state of constant fighting for another century. As a consequence, both kingdoms kept losing the power and stability they once had.

In Israel, Jehu died and was succeeded by his son, Jehoahaz. This king appeared to be incompetent, but all that the biblical text says about him is that he repeats the sins of Jeroboam and worships "pagan" deities.[lxxvii] As a punishment—or by coincidence—the devastation of the Kingdom of Israel begins during the reign of this king.

The Arameans Invade Israel

First, the Arameans sacked Israel. Hazael, the king of Aram, and his son, Ben-Hadad, invaded Israel and captured several cities. Then they returned to their land, leaving unimaginable damage behind. Jehoahaz's army was reduced to ten thousand footmen, no more than fifty horsemen, and ten chariots.

The End of Jehu's Dynasty

Jehoahaz was succeeded by his son Joash, also known as Jehoash, who fought the Kingdom of Judah during the reign of Amaziah, capturing him—and a ton of wealth from the Temple of Jerusalem—and then defeated Ben-Hadad of Aram. The next ruler after Jehoash was his son, Jeroboam II.

Jeroboam's son, Zechariah, was killed in treachery. His murderer, Shallum, sat on the throne of Israel for a month, before being killed by Menahem. This Menahem and his son, Pekahiah, were among the cruelest and overall worst kings that Israel ever had. Pekahiah was killed by Pekah, who ruled for twenty years and during that time attacked Judah.[lxxviii]

Good and Bad Kings of Judah

During Jeroboam's reign in Israel, the rightful king Azariah started ruling Judah and remained on the throne for fifty-two years. After he died of leprosy (and very old age), his son Jotham took his place and continued the same just rule. Jotham rebuilt a gate of the Temple that had been damaged earlier by Pekah's army and the Arameans. After his death, Jotham was succeeded by his son, Ahaz.

Just like Menahem in Israel, Ahaz did some outrageous things as the king of Judah. He even sacrificed one of his sons to a local deity. In fact, there was a whole sanctuary where people burned ther children as a sacrifice.

Assyrian Conquest and Depopulation of Israel

When the Aramean king Rezin and Israel's King Pekah attacked Judah, Ahaz asked the Assyrian king Tiglath-pileser for help. The Assyrian army came and devastated Ahaz's enemies, capturing Damascus and many of Israel's cities. Tiglath-pileser killed King Rezin of Aram, and Pekah was dethroned (or killed) in Israel.

The Assyrian king demonstrated his power by sending Israelites into exile and by appointing Hoshea as the new king of Israel. Hoshea, however, rebelled against this new master, hoping to receive some backup from Egypt. This never happened, so Hoshea remained alone, unable to resist the Assyrian conquerors.

Tiglath-pileser had already substituted the entire population of Israel with other peoples that inhabited his vast empire. The Israelites were moved without a trace. The next two Assyrian kings—Shalmaneser V and Sargon II—seized and destroyed every remaining Israelite city, including Samaria. The ten tribes that formed the Kingdom of Israel were now lost forever, and they are still referred to as the "ten lost tribes."

Chapter 12 – Judah's Resistance and Reforms

The people of Judah were shocked to find out that Israel had been devastated. These new circumstances made the Kingdom of Judah considerably vulnerable. It became clear that the people of this tribe may have shared the same destiny as the northern ones—they were not unbeatable after all. Judah's rulers realized it was their last chance to consolidate, save the kingdom and its people, and prevent the destruction that struck their northern neighbors. Their efforts brought results for a while, as the kingdom endured for another 150 years.

The new king of Judah, Ahaz's son Hezekiah, and his great-grandson Josiah two generations later changed the way Judah was governed. Both kings were devoted to God (although Hezekiah's immediate successor was not) and they did their best to save Judah from imminent destruction.

Hezekiah, the Good King

Hezekiah showed his devotion to the Jewish God by razing the alternate sites of worship, dedicated to Baal and other local deities, to the ground throughout the Kingdom of Judah. He went so far that he completely destroyed the serpent that Moses made of bronze so that he could heal the people bitten by venomous snakes in the wilderness.[lxxix] To make sure his decisions were always aligned with God's plan, he invited the prophet Isaiah to advise him.

Even though Hezekiah had made profound religious and political reforms, Judah suffered defeat after defeat. The Assyrians overwhelmed the kingdom and invaded forty-six cities, including Lachish.[lxxx] But the enemy aimed to capture Jerusalem.

"Angel" Saves Jerusalem

The Assyrian king, Sennacherib, threatened King Hezekiah, saying that he would destroy his land and kill him unless he surrendered. Hezekiah was desperate and asked God to help him. Eventually, the prophet Isaiah said everything was going to be fine—God was going to save Jerusalem this time.

Assyrians were getting ready to attack Jerusalem in the morning, but during the night, all of them—some 185,000 men—suddenly died. The Bible claims it's because an angel visited their camp. Other ancient sources confirm that a large number of soldiers died that night. Herodotus wrote that the Assyrians were stricken by the plague. Also, a royal inscription found around the remains of King Sennacherib's palace says that the Assyrian king had sieged Jerusalem and trapped the king of Judah like a caged bird, but that was it. The Assyrians never made their threats come true.

Manasseh and Amon

The reign of Hezekiah's son, Manasseh, was notably long (forty-five years) and stable. However, this king annulled his father's religious reforms, and the biblical authors condemn him. So, we are not given much detail on how he managed to rule so effectively to enjoy such a long period of power. Instead, we are informed that he practiced witchcraft, took advice from mediums, put a carved image of the goddess Asherah in the Temple, and even sacrificed one of his children to a foreign god. The whole population of Judah seemed to follow the king and turn away from God, and God promised that the end of Judah was near.[lxxxi] Also, we should not forget that constant warfare devastated both the economy and population of Judah—and outside of the kingdom, there were new military super forces such as Babylon.

Manasseh died of old age, and his son, Amon, became king. However, Amon made some unpopular decisions and had no public support whatsoever. After only two years, he was killed by his own officials. The only person suitable to succeed him was his eight-year-old son Josiah.

The Pious King Josiah

Josiah followed the path of his great-grandfather Hezekiah and carried out a profound religious reform toward monotheism. Early in his reign, priests found a scroll containing the Law of Moses in the Temple. Josiah listened to a priest read the Law; he then deeply repented for not being aware of the law, and started destroying all newly built altars of foreign deities—including a large altar that Jeroboam built in Bethel in the former Kingdom of Israel.[lxxxii]

Not surprisingly, Josiah is highly praised by biblical authors and deeply mourned by subsequent prophets, such as Jeremiah, when he was killed by Egyptians.[lxxxiii]

Chapter 13 – The Fall of Jerusalem and the End of the Kingdom of Judah

Two powerful empires—Egypt and Babylon—threatened to annihilate the Kingdom of Judah entirely. After he had killed Josiah, the Egyptian Pharaoh Neco captured Josiah's son, King Jehoahaz, and replaced him with his brother Jehoiakim, who was now to serve the pharaoh as Egypt's vassal. The new king of Judah taxed the people to pay the tribute in gold and silver to the pharaoh.

However, Egypt did not remain the top player for long. King Nebuchadnezzar of Babylon started conquering all the nearby lands quickly and almost effortlessly, gaining a considerable advantage. When the Babylonian army neared Jerusalem, Jehoiakim changed sides and supported Nebuchadnezzar against the Egyptian pharaoh.

A couple of years later, however, Nebuchadnezzar failed to invade Egypt and retreated. Jehoiakim believed it was the right moment to set the Kingdom of Judah free from Babylonian claws and he rebelled against the foreign power. Nebuchadnezzar was infuriated; first, he decided to devastate the Egyptian army, and then he instructed his forces to attack Jerusalem and kill King Jehoiakim. It was the beginning of the end, as nothing was going to save Jerusalem this time.

The King Surrenders

After Jehoiakim's death, his son, Jehoiachin, ruled in his place, but he only ruled for just three months. Nebuchadnezzar laid siege to Jerusalem, and the king surrendered himself. King Jehoiachin, as well as his family, officials, and a ton of treasures from his palace and the Temple, were taken away and brought to Babylon. The city of Jerusalem was not ruined at this point, but over 10,000 people were exiled. Only some of the poorest remained in the city, and they suffered as the next ten years were marked by poor economy and terrible famine.[lxxxiv]

Final Destruction

Nebuchadnezzar placed Zedekiah, Jehoiachin's uncle, on the throne of Judah, so that he could ensure the taxes are being collected. Zedekiah was not happy with the status of a vassal king, and after a couple of years, he rebelled against Nebuchadnezzar. Babylon responded harshly. The army of Nebuchadnezzar besieged Jerusalem for two years before breaking into the city. The Babylonians captured King Zedekiah and killed all his sons before his eyes. That's the last scene he would ever see; having killed the king's sons, the Babylonians stabbed Zedekiah's eyes out and took him to Babylon in chains.

Within a short time span, Nebuchadnezzar deported the remaining population of Judah and devastated the city of Jerusalem of all its fortifications, the royal palace, and the Temple. For almost forty years, Solomon's Temple in Jerusalem was the heart of Israelite faith symbolizing its resilience. Its destruction represented the end of an era.

Conclusion

Even though the Assyrians and Babylonians had put an end to the Israelite kingdoms, the story of Jewish people and their devotion to God didn't end with the sack of Jerusalem and the destruction of the Temple.

Less than a century later, Babylon was conquered by the Persians. The Judean exiles were now at the mercy of the Persian King Cyrus, who was much more generous than Nebuchadnezzar. Cyrus respected the Judeans and their religion and even said he was instructed by God to let the exiles back home, to rebuild their holiest city and the Temple. He even provided the means for them to return to their land and start over.

After seven decades of exile in Babylon, the people of Judah returned to Jerusalem, renovate the city, recreate the Temple, and begin their relationship with God again. During that period, their scholars—priests and scribes—write extensively about the Golden Age of Jerusalem, and the kings of the united monarchy, especially David and Solomon.

Much later, various segments of these immortal stories are found in oral traditions of many nations. Epic heroes of medieval Europe look just like David, and their wise kings make judgments just the way Solomon did in the Bible. That's why it is important to know where these familiar stories originally came from, to find out all that we didn't know.

The history of the kings of ancient Israel and Judah is not just a part of the history of one nation. It is at the heart of the history of the Western world. Religious people of the three major religions—Judaism, Christianity, and Islam—see these people and events as undisputed truth. Non-religious people have been exposed to these ideas as well. These are the ancient stories that form our views of power, religion, leadership, wars, courage and cowardice, nations and individuals, loyalty and betrayal, virtue and sin, monotheism and magic—not to mention the whole art history that is full with various biblical motives.

No one of us knows everything about the history of the world. There are many parts of that mosaic, and the history of Israelite and Judean kings surely is an essential one.

Timeline of the Kings of Israel and Judah

c. 1025 – 1010 BCE   King Saul rules.

c. 1010 – 970 BCE   King David rules.

c. 1000 BCE King David makes Jerusalem the capital of the United Kingdom

c. 970 – 931 BCE King Solomon rules.

c. 960 BCE Solomon completes the Temple in Jerusalem.

c. 931 BCE Divide between the Kingdom of Israel (with capital in Samaria) and the Kingdom of Judah (with capital in Jerusalem).

c. 740 – 722 BCE Assyrians conquer the Kingdom of Israel.

597 BCE First deportation of the Israelites to Babylon.

586 BCE Nebuchadnezzar conquers Jerusalem and destroys Solomon's Temple.

Timeline of Kings during the Divided Monarchy

Kings of Judah Kings of Israel

Rehoboam (928–911) Jeroboam I (928–907)

Abijam or Abijam (911–908) Nadab (907–906)

Asa (908–867) Baasha (906–883)

Jehoshaphat (870–846) Eliah (883–882); Zimri (882)

Jehoram or Joram (851–843) Omri (882–871)

Ahaziah or Jehoahaz (843–842) Ahab (873–852)

Athaliah (842–836)   Ahaziah (852–851)

Jehoash or Joash (836–798)   Jehoram or Joram (851–842)

Amaziah (798–769) Jehu (842–814)

Azariah or Uzziah (785-733) Jehoahaz (817–800)

Jotham (759–743) Jehoash or Joash (800–784)

Ahaz (743–715) Jeroboam II (788–747)

Hezekiah (715–687) Zechariah (747); Shallum (747)

Manasseh (687–642) Menahem (747–737)

Amon (641–640) Pekahiah (737–732)

Josiah (640–609) Pekah (735–732)

Jehoahaz (609) Hoshea (732–722)

Jehoiakim (608–598)

Jehoiachin (597)

Zedekiah (597–586)

Part 3: Queen of Sheba

A Captivating Guide to a Mysterious Queen Mentioned in the Bible and Her Relationship with King Solomon

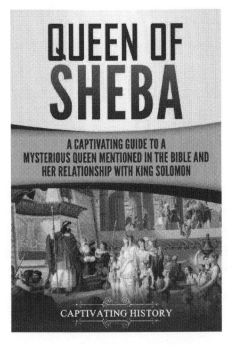

Introduction

Writing a biography for the Queen of Sheba is quickly complicated by a simple roadblock: the fact that historians aren't sure that this mysterious queen ever even existed.

To start with, the events detailed in the story of the queen took place so long ago that written records of that time and place barely exist except in the form of religious manuscripts. The Queen of Sheba reigned around 950 BCE, nearly 3,000 years ago, and written records from the areas where Sheba could have existed are few and far between. The records we do have telling the story of the queen come from three major religions: Islam, Christianity, and Judaism. In the holy texts from these religions—including the *Kebra Nagast* from Ethiopia, the Hebrew Bible's Books of Chronicles, the Holy Bible, the Quran, and the Jewish Antiquities—accounts of the Queen of Sheba center on one major event in her life: her visit with King Solomon of Israel. Even here, the accounts differ wildly on what exactly the nature of her encounter with the wise king was.

The most detailed record of the queen's life lies in the *Kebra Nagast*. This Ethiopian text, whose title translates to "The Glory of Kings," is also of unknown origin; however, it was intensely important to Ethiopian emperors of the Solomonic dynasty and became an integral part of Orthodox Christianity in Ethiopia. In this book, the

Queen of Sheba's visit to King Solomon morphs from a quest for wisdom into a romantic encounter, and it eventually results in a union that would produce a dynasty that lasted for millennia. Ancient Ethiopian mythology also mentions a courageous warrior maiden, a virgin who faced down despicable monsters and who bore the same name—and existed in the same timeframe—as the Queen of Sheba mentioned in the holy texts.

Archaeological evidence, however, barely points to an existence of Sheba at all, let alone providing any evidence of a queen somewhere along its timeline.

Piecing together an account of the queen's life from these varied sources gives one a fascinating glimpse into the ancient world, and from the turmoil of this chaos of information rises one constant figure: the queen herself. In every account, she is bold and wise, fearless and selfless. She strives to bring peace and protection to her country. She faces monsters on behalf of the innocent masses, and she finds herself in power even though female rulers were rare in her era. And instead of backing away from the responsibility, she seizes it with two hands. She travels the world seeking wisdom, and when she finds love instead, she has the courage to unselfishly turn her back on that love and journey back to a home that she has promised to care for. At every turn, the Queen of Sheba remains one of the earliest symbols of female power, and her story—her legend—still serves to be a fascinating and inspiring one, one that speaks to hearts and minds even today, whether it is myth or history.

Chapter 1 – Sheba Before the Queen

The first thing that we don't really know about the Queen of Sheba is where exactly Sheba was. Historians have been puzzling for generations over the location of this mysterious land; considering that the queen herself visited Solomon in around 950 BCE, it's no easy question to answer. Guesses have included Yemen, southern Arabia, and parts of Africa. However, the legends and traditions that include the most detail and that align most closely with the biblical account of the Queen of Sheba point to Sheba being one of the oldest kingdoms in the entire world: Ethiopia.

An Ancient Nation

Ethiopia is the oldest independent country on the African continent. Its rich history goes back for thousands of years, with one of its most prominent beginnings being the Kingdom of Aksum in 100 CE. But Ethiopia's story begins much, much earlier than that. According to the story of the Queen of Sheba, this unique and ancient country was already a vast and wealthy nation a thousand years before the name of Aksum would ever be spoken. This is unsurprising considering that Ethiopia may be one of the first places in the world to be inhabited by human beings. It is speculated that the Garden of Eden itself may have been located somewhere in Ethiopia, and science has proven that some of the earliest human tribes lived in this beautiful and ancient country.

The furthest reaches of the history of Ethiopia have long since been lost to the 3,000 years between the Queen of Sheba's reign and the modern day. The earliest mentions of this kingdom come from the same book that describes the Queen of Sheba's visit to Solomon: The Holy Bible.

The Origins of Ethiopia According to the Bible

The Book of Genesis details the creation of the world and of mankind itself. It also tells the story of how the first two children born in the newly minted universe—Cain and Abel, the two sons of Adam—divided the human race in half when it was still in its very infancy. Cast out of the Garden of Eden because of the sins of Adam and his wife Eve, the world's first family found themselves tilling the earth to survive. A bout of jealousy rose up between the two brothers, and in a fit of terrible rage, Cain killed his own brother. The world's first murder had been committed.

According to the Bible and to an ancient Ethiopian Christian text, the *Kebra Nagast*, which contains the most detailed account of the life of the Queen of Sheba, the descendants of Cain and Seth, their younger brother who followed in Abel's footsteps, remained divided. While the descendants of Seth became leaders, the descendants of Cain developed into barbaric nations, eventually becoming so unutterably abominable in the sight of God that they were washed away in the Great Flood. Only a descendant of Seth—Noah—and his family survived.

It is here, right after the description of the Great Flood, where we find the origin of Ethiopia itself according to these two ancient texts. According to the King James Bible:

> Now these are the generations of the sons of Noah, Shem, Ham, and Japheth: and unto them were sons born after the flood. [...] By these were the isles of the Gentiles divided in

their lands; everyone after his tongue, after their families, in their nations. And the sons of Ham; **Cush**, and Mizraim, and Phut, and Canaan. And the sons of **Cush**; Seba, and Havilah, and Sabtah, and Raamah, and Sabtechah: and the sons of Raamah; **Sheba**, and Dedan.

– Genesis 10:1 and 5-9

"Cush" is an ancient name for Ethiopia, and as this passage notes that nations grew from these prominent families, it is easy to imagine that Ethiopia may have developed from the descendants of Cush. In fact, a group of languages still spoken in Ethiopia today is still referred to as the "Cushitic languages." Somewhere along the line, Cush's descendant Sheba may have loaned his name to the nation that would be formed by his offspring, and so the Sheba whose queen became so famous might have been born.

Sheba and D'mt

The very first mention of Ethiopia is found in the hieroglyphs of the ancient Egyptians, dating back to about 2500 BCE. There it is spoken of as the land of Punt, a country where Egyptian merchants were able to find an abundance of trade, particularly in gold. The exact location of Punt has not been ascertained, but it was likely somewhere in the northern regions of modern-day Ethiopia.

Fast forward several hundred years into the Iron Age, and one finds the first confirmed kingdom that was established in the area of Ethiopia. Details about this kingdom are sketchy and shadowy, wreathed in the mists of distant history, but its name survives: D'mt. It was likely formed somewhere between 1000 and 700 BCE, and even the nature of its inhabitants remains a mystery to this day. While many of them were likely indigenous people from the area, there was also probably a high proportion of Sabaean people. The Sabaeans were a south Arabic people from an area of modern-day Yemen, another region which has also been proposed as being the Sheba of the Bible, although its accounts of the Queen of Sheba are not as richly detailed as that of the Ethiopians.

D'mt itself may have been the kingdom ruled over by the Queen of Sheba herself or was possibly even a neighboring kingdom; Sheba and D'mt, at any rate, existed at the same time, although they may not have been the same kingdom. The people of D'mt left only a few inscriptions behind, and even fewer archaeological expeditions have been conducted in order to find out more about this ancient kingdom. Their legacy lives on mostly in the ruins of mighty temples built from impressive stone.

Sheba at the Time of the Queen

Only one thing can be known for certain about the Kingdom of Sheba at the time when its famous queen was born: it had to have been rich—inexpressibly rich. Considering that it was conveniently located on a trade route that would have put it in touch with powers such as ancient Egypt and the might of Israel, this is no great surprise. Ethiopia was also a land rich in all kinds of natural resources with great stretches of fertile land and gold running rich in its rivers and earth. It was into this rich and flourishing land—somewhere in the 10th century BCE—that the legendary queen would be born. Yet abundant though her surroundings must have been, the queen's ascension to the throne could not have been easy. For she became queen the same way that all monarchs ascended in those days: by a death in the family.

Chapter 2 – The Shadow of the Serpent King

Awre towered above the city of Aksum, the scaly length of his terrifying body rising above the buildings, screams echoing from wall to wall as his slender shadow fell across the length and breadth of the entire city. His jaws gaped open, great fangs curving from them, a crown glittering on his flat head above two brilliant eyes that were frighteningly human in the face of a monstrous snake. A forked tongue stabbed at the sky, moving as swift and sinuous as the curves of the monster as Awre slithered through the streets, his foul breath preceding him like a portent of the deaths that were to come.

The people of Aksum didn't think. They just grabbed their children and fled. They all knew that dreaded silhouette on the horizon far too well—Awre had been terrorizing the city for years, devouring livestock by the hundreds. Cattle and sheep, camels and chickens—they were all the same to Awre's insatiable appetite. But on this day, the people fled with a special fear in their hearts. A fear that was for more than just their livestock.

Awre's lashing tail smashed into the corner of a building. Crumbling stone rained down on the street, and a young mother screamed, snatching up her little daughter out of the path of the falling debris. She stared up at the shape of the monster as it went past and cowered into the niche of the doorway, clutching her little girl as tightly as she could. She knew what day it was. She knew that someone's daughter was about to be taken. Because despite the vast number of animals that Awre consumed, their flesh was not enough for the serpent king. Once a year, he demanded something more, a special treat to allay his bloodthirst: the sacrifice of a human being—and not just any human being, but a pure and beautiful virgin girl.

Now, he continued down the streets, his deep laugh rocking the foundations of the houses as he slithered eagerly toward his annual feast. He saw her silhouette waiting for him on a designated hilltop. Her curves were as slender as his were scaly, but even from this distance, he could see that there was something different about her. The girls normally screamed and wept. This one stood on the top of the hill with her feet planted wide apart and her arms folded, and as he drew closer, he saw something burning brightly in her eyes. It wasn't fear. It was fire.

The girl's skin blazed like ebony in the midday sun, her brown eyes were alight, and her shining black hair was swept back and pinned down by the weight of her bejeweled tiara. Surprised, the serpent king came to a halt, rising up so that he stood over his quarry. She met his eyes with a defiance that he had never seen before.

"Makeda, the Princess of Sheba?" Awre was as surprised as he was amused. "If your people think that sacrificing a young woman so beautiful and of such high rank will sate my appetite for longer than the usual year, they are sadly mistaken." He lowered his head, his forked tongue flicking out only inches from her beautiful face. "Yet I will not deny that you will make a wonderful meal."

Makeda raised her chin. There was nothing but cool determination in her face. "I will make your last one," she murmured.

Awre laughed. Then he reared back his head, opened his jaws wide, and struck. So did Makeda. With the swiftness of the serpent that she hoped to conquer, she grasped the ugly horn that curled from the tip of his snout. Her hand reached into the front of her dress and pulled out a dagger that cut the sunshine with its sharpness. The dagger flashed, and blood burst down the front of Awre's throat. The serpent king reared back, ripping his horn from Makeda's hands, and he tried to take a deep breath to roar, but his throat was cut. He could not even scream in pain. He just fell backward and collapsed, the whole terrible length of him falling at Makeda's feet. Sheba was saved from his scourge forever.

* * * *

The birthday of the Queen of Sheba has been lost, as has most of the details about her childhood. All we really have is this legend about a girl named Makeda, a name meaning *not thus*; perhaps because she would later become known for converting her people from their indigenous faith (which, according to the Quran, was the worship of the sun) to monotheism, likely Judaism. She probably earned the name by telling the people that "not thus is it good (to worship the sun or stars)," pointing them in the direction of monotheism instead.

All this, however, was far in the future. Princess Makeda probably did not single-handedly slay a monstrous monarch, but the fable must have arisen from a young woman of exceptional fortitude and resourcefulness. As a princess, Makeda had already proven herself to be an intelligent and determined young woman who knew what she wanted and would stop at nothing to get it, especially when it came to protecting her people.

Her early life in the royal capital of Sheba (which might have been modern-day Yeha, as evidenced by numerous ruins built by the people of D'mt) was a privileged one. Sheba was a ridiculously wealthy kingdom made rich by an abundance of gold, spices, and other priceless treasures carried off by its merchants to other great powers of the ancient world. Makeda had everything she could have possibly wanted, and with her father on the throne, her future was stable.

Or so she thought. In the ancient world, kingdoms were often ruled over by kings and not by queens. Compared to their male counterparts, queens had very little power. Wars were fought and alliances made by the kings of all the countries who had absolute power over all of their subjects, including their royal wives. Having a queen on the throne without a king was unthinkable, but it was about to happen and in a manner that would bring tragedy to Makeda's young life.

It is likely that Makeda was still a young woman when the current king of Sheba either died or was somehow removed from the throne, probably in an unexpected manner. The end of his reign threatened to cast the entire kingdom of Sheba into chaos. With no one to lead them, what would become of the people? Their riches were a liability now, with power-hungry rulers on every side ready to invade and plunder the coffers that Makeda's father had worked so hard to protect. If a strong ruler failed to take the throne, Sheba and its people would be doomed.

So, Makeda did what she was fabled to have done on the hilltops of Aksum. She saw that her people were in trouble. And she stepped up to protect them. She was crowned the Queen of Sheba and suddenly became possibly the most powerful woman in all of her known world.

Chapter 3 – A Questioning Queen

Illustration I: The Queen of Sheba as depicted in a 15th-century illuminated manuscript

Now on the throne of the mighty nation of Sheba, Makeda had restored stability and security to her country simply by her ascension. It appears that Sheba continued to prosper during her reign; trade was bustling, and the country's mines continued to overflow with abundant gold.

Yet the young queen was not wholly content upon her throne. She had never been raised to rule a kingdom—she lacked the lifelong education that a young man in her position would have received in being groomed for kingship as the crown prince. Now, although she maintained admirable control over Sheba, Makeda longed desperately for a mentor. She had no one to ask when she was uncertain about something, no experience to fall back on when difficult decisions came her way, and as the ruling queen, difficult decisions were a daily part of her job description.

There was something else that Makeda yearned for, too, although this was a more subconscious longing. Her mind and sense of duty wanted a mentor, someone to guide her through all of the twists and turns that her queenly path was taking. But her heart had needs and desires of its own.

Little did she know that, 2,000 miles away, her heart's desire was waiting on the throne of Jerusalem.

* * * *

King Solomon had big shoes to fill.

His father was David—a name that had become legendary long before David ever became king. A shepherd boy who had become a killer of giants, a renowned warrior, a mighty king, and "a man after God's own heart," King David was the golden boy of the golden age of Israel. He led the nation out of the darkness of King Saul's reign, despite Saul's multiple attempts to murder him, and David's long reign had been illustrious.

Solomon was not King David's firstborn son. Instead, he was the result of King David's greatest mistake: committing adultery with a beautiful woman named Bathsheba and having her husband killed in battle so that he could marry her. Solomon should have been a pariah, an outcast, a scapegoat for the sins of his father. Instead, according to Nathan the Prophet, Solomon was God's favorite among David's children. David accepted Nathan's prophecy and groomed Solomon to become the heir to his throne, and when age and infirmity confined David to his bedchamber, Solomon was crowned King of Israel.

It had been years now since Solomon had taken the throne. The early days of his rule had not been easy with conspirators rising up against him and even his own older brother trying to seize power, but Solomon had succeeded in establishing himself as the king. And he was proving himself to be a king unlike any other. According to the Bible, God had appeared to Solomon in a dream, asking him what he wanted: "Ask what I shall give thee."

Solomon could have asked for anything. Power, wealth, glory—but instead, the young king wanted only one thing: wisdom. "Give therefore thy servant an understanding heart to judge thy people, that I may discern between good and bad: for who is able to judge this thy so great a people?" he asked. His prayer was answered, and Solomon's wisdom became renowned throughout the ancient world.

Now, Solomon was reigning comfortably over his vast nation. While he had failed to ask God for wealth when he'd given his request for wisdom, he had become almost immeasurably rich. Thousands of chariot horses pranced in his stables; Egypt and Philistia, the historical enemies of Israel, now paid him tribute. Times of peace and plenty had come, and Solomon was able to turn his mind to a mission that had been given to him even before he was born.

David had always wanted to build a great temple to the God of Israel, but God had forbidden him from doing so because David was a man of war, instead telling David that he would give the task to his son since he would be a peaceful ruler. While Solomon was a great king, the same as his father was, this was where much of the similarities between the two men ended. History knows them best by their writings, which is a great example of the differences between them. David wrote the Psalms, an emotive, passionate, often desperate collection of songs whose lyrics are often raw. Solomon, on the other hand, wrote the Proverbs, which soberly sets out wise instructions for his son. Wild and warlike David may have forged a kingdom, but he was not fit to build the first and most wonderful temple in Jerusalem.

Solomon, on the other hand, was as intelligent and grounded as he was wise, and he knew that building this temple would be his duty. So, he started to gather the materials for the temple, and this was a task that could have only been performed by this wealthiest of kings. He would need wood, gold, priceless fabrics, precious stones, and shining metals in almost unimaginable proportions. And he would need to search the farthest reaches of the known world in order to find everything he needed. He would search throughout Israel, even into Egypt and Assyria, and perhaps even across the Mediterranean.

Perhaps even as far as Sheba.

Chapter 4 – Word of the Wise King

Tamrin had been all over the known world. He had walked the Silk Road to the borders of China, bringing back priceless Asian treasures to his beloved queen; wandered the barren deserts of Arabia; beheld the majesty of the pyramids and the riches of the pharaohs; and lived in the magnificence that was Sheba at the time of Queen Makeda. Yet the one place that he hadn't yet seen was Israel. Tamrin was an educated merchant, and he'd heard much about the place. It was a strange country, he had learned, a place where all of its citizens worshiped only one god, and where there were no astrologers, no magicians, and no soothsayers allowed. As his dhows, some of the swiftest cargo ships in the world, parted the waters of the Red Sea, Tamrin gazed to the east, eagerly anticipating his first sighting of this new land.

Israel had never been on his usual trade route before. In fact, it was a promising—and mysterious—request that brought him in this direction. Solomon, the peculiar but extremely wealthy king of Israel, had sent out a request to merchants all over the world asking for their most precious and expensive materials in huge quantities. He had gold and silver aplenty, he said; he wanted building materials, and only the very best would do. Alloys of gold mixed with copper so that it gleamed red. Sapphires. Ebony. Tamrin had seen splendid buildings in Sheba, and he had handled almost incomprehensibly valuable cargoes before, but the reason behind this king's request was puzzling. Solomon wanted to build a temple—a gigantic, magnificent temple, even bigger and more beautiful than his own royal palace.

Tamrin didn't understand, but he did recognize a business opportunity when he saw one. And so, when King Solomon's request had reached him, he didn't hesitate to set sail for Israel with his dhows wallowing low in the water, laden heavily with every treasure he could find within the borders of Sheba and along the rest of his trade route. His was one of the largest fleets of all of Sheba with more than seventy ships surrounding his own, all of them bearing expensive cargo. He could only hope that this Israelite king was as rich as he seemed to think he was.

When Tamrin arrived in Jerusalem, the capital of Israel and the seat of its king, he realized that the accounts of Solomon's wealth and wisdom had not been exaggerated. The port where he left his dhows had been utterly teeming with merchant vessels; his short journey inland to Jerusalem itself had taken him through fields of growing crops with fattened cattle grazing on all of the hills. Approaching Jerusalem had been as awe-inspiring as it was intimidating. The city towered above the rest of the landscape, resting on a rocky hill. Its walls and buttresses were imposing, the gleaming armor of its soldiers a threat to any who dared to oppose it. These soldiers were battle-hardened veterans, too; Tamrin had seen many with scars, relics from the terrible wars that King David had fought against the Philistines and other enemies. More recently, a civil war had gripped the country when David's own son Absalom had risen up against him.

But Absalom was long gone now. The Philistines had been reduced to tributaries, and Solomon had taken Absalom's place as heir to the throne. The soldiers stood motionless and idle, their weapons sheathed, and the city gates had been thrown wide open to the stream of merchants making their laborious way up the hills. Mules and donkeys, camels and oxen, filled the road, all of them bearing heavy loads of wonderful materials in such abundance that Tamrin could only stare. His hundreds of camels were not the only beasts of burden to carry expensive goods up this hill. Leading his caravan, Tamrin sneaked glances at the other merchants around him. The animals were carrying ingots of bronze, great rolls of purple fabric, and planks of Lebanon cedar. Whatever reasons this king had for building a temple, he was going to build a truly magnificent one.

When Tamrin reached Solomon's palace, he already felt like his eyeballs might fall out of his head from staring. The streets of Jerusalem were filled with people, and they all seemed to be so happy; there was music on every street corner, laughing vendors doing brisk business with chattering women, and children chasing one another through the streets. The palace itself was an awesome sight, its towering pillars richly decorated with all kinds of precious metals and brilliant fabrics.

Once Tamrin's camels and their burdens had been taken care of, he made his way into the palace where he was received by Solomon himself. The king had decided to personally oversee all of the operations regarding the building of the temple, and that included speaking to the merchants that had brought materials from far-off lands. Tamrin realized that he was nervous about meeting this famous king, which surprised him; as a personal friend of Queen Makeda, he was no stranger to royalty. But there was something a little terrifying about the wealth and power that was evident in Solomon's court. He wiped his sweating hands on his robes before daring to approach the throne room.

The room itself was dazzling beyond compare. The steps leading up to the throne were decorated with golden lions, and the floor gleamed in shining marble. The king who sat upon the throne was broad-shouldered, his beard tumbling to his chest, the line of his jaw as stern and formidable as the walls surrounding his palace. Yet, when Tamrin bowed low, the voice that told him to rise held a gentleness that he hadn't been expecting. He looked into the king's eyes for the first time and was surprised to see humility there. Solomon's speech was gentle, and when he sent a servant girl to bring wine and bread to the tired merchant, his request was spoken softly. A little speechless, Tamrin automatically went through the motions of discussing the merchandise that he had brought to Solomon and negotiating a price, but his mind was occupied with other things.

Firstly, he had been all over the world but never stepped foot in a kingdom quite like Solomon's Israel. And secondly, Queen Makeda had told him how much she had wanted to find a mentor that could guide her through the monumental task of governing a kingdom like Sheba. Tamrin was pretty sure he'd just stumbled upon the perfect person for that task.

Chapter 5 – A Journey to Israel

Tamrin had been back for a few days already, and all he ever spoke of was the wisdom of King Solomon.

Queen Makeda, who was a friend of the merchant, received him every morning to hear more about his travels all the way to Jerusalem and back. At first, she was slightly amused by the enthusiasm with which Tamrin spoke of the grand country he had visited, its incredible architecture, its happy people, and most of all, /its wise king. Tamrin was usually not one to gush, as he was a weathered, seasoned, battle-scarred man who had seen it all and survived everything. Yet there was a light in his eyes that Makeda had never seen before, and after a few days of listening to his stories, it began to fascinate her. She found herself asking about everything he'd seen, and there was one part of all his stories that interested her more than anything else: Solomon.

Makeda knew that Tamrin had done business with most of the great powers of her ancient world. Yet he had never seemed so awestruck before as he was now. What struck Makeda the most was that Tamrin was impressed with King Solomon not for his wealth or his good looks or his military prowess—in fact, Tamrin said, King

Solomon had never once been to war. Instead, the merchant was awed by the king's wisdom. In an age when world leaders came to power based solely on their parentage, foolish kings were in abundance. Many of the monarchs in power at the time were selfish, power-hungry, and occasionally even insane. But not Solomon, Tamrin told Makeda. He was more than just a good king—he held a wisdom, a depth of knowledge and intelligence that Tamrin had never seen before. As much as Solomon's coffers overflowed with gold, Tamrin told the queen, his mind overflowed with wisdom. His judgments were always just, yet there was a humility in him, a willingness to learn from others and a gentleness in his dealings with his servants, that was rare to see in people of any rank.

The more that Tamrin talked about Solomon, the more Makeda became enamored with this king that she had never met. While all was going well in her kingdom, she was still feeling lost and alone in her haughty position. There was no one to guide her, no princely education to draw upon; Makeda felt like she was winging it, flying blind with the fate of her people at stake. Solomon seemed to be the opposite of her. He had grown up in the shadow of the mightiest king that Israel had ever had, and he seemed to be so sure of this God that his people served. If what he said was true, this God of his had given him wisdom that surpassed anything even the well-traveled Tamrin had seen before. Makeda wasn't so sure of this God of Israel, but she was sure of one thing: Tamrin was different after spending time with Solomon, and she wanted whatever it was that Solomon had that made him capable of ruling with such calm confidence.

Every day, Makeda summoned Tamrin up to her palace and listened to everything that he had to say, her eyes wide and rapt as she hung on his every word. Sometimes she cried when Tamrin told her of the things that Solomon had done and said. Tamrin assumed that she was just awed and took pleasure in the things that he said, but perhaps there was something else that caused the queen to weep, something more inconsolable: a desperate yearning to be able to do what Solomon could do. Makeda wanted to rule better, and she wanted to know the answers to the deep questions in her heart, questions that she could no longer ask of her parents because they were gone.

At last, after listening to hundreds of Tamrin's stories about his time in Jerusalem, Makeda made up her mind. Everything was peaceful and stable in Sheba, but it might not always remain that way. She needed to learn more about how to be a good monarch and how to care for her people well. There were no two ways about it: The Queen of Sheba had to meet King Solomon. No matter how arduous the journey might be, Makeda was determined to make it, for the good of her kingdom.

* * * *

Queen Makeda faced the crowds of her people, her heart fluttering with nervousness. She knew by the adoration in their eyes that they placed their trust in her, yet part of her was terrified by their trust, feeling in her heart that she was unworthy of it. But they couldn't know that. They had to believe in a strong and courageous queen, so she kept her back straight and her chin up as she addressed them.

"Hearken, O ye who are my people," she began, "and give ye ear to my words. For I desire wisdom..."

The people listened attentively, every eye and ear fixed upon their queen as she spoke. She had worked hard on her speech, and she gave it with confidence, telling them about the riches and goodness of the wisdom that she sought after so earnestly. She spoke of its sweetness, its strength, and its value, calling it "the best of all treasures." "I will follow in the footprints of wisdom, and she shall protect me forever," Queen Makeda told her people. "I will seek after wisdom, and she shall be with me forever."

Her voice grew softer as she went on, and a wistful quality crept into them as she began to extol the virtues of a wise person. "By the sight of him thou shalt become wise," she said. "Hearken to the utterance of his mouth, so that thou mayest become like unto him." She lowered her eyes, longing creeping into her tone. "And I love him merely on hearing concerning him," she almost whispered, "and without seeing him, and the whole story of him that hath been told to me is to me as the desire of my heart, and like water to the thirsty man."

Silence fell, and Makeda's heart flipped over. The last sentence she'd spoken had been almost to herself; it was not a part of the speech that she had so carefully planned. She froze, holding her breath as her people gazed at her. Had they seen the emotion that had suddenly overtaken her? Did they think her weak?

But her people's reaction was favorable. They admired her commitment to seeking out more knowledge, and they pledged their loyalty to her and their dedication to whichever cause she saw fit to invest her time in. Makeda, hugely relieved, at once started to make preparations to leave. This was no small task. As the queen of a powerful and wealthy country like Sheba, Makeda knew that she had to arrive in Jerusalem with a suitable amount of majesty and ceremony. She was the ultimate ambassador for Sheba, and it was her duty to show off its strength as well as she could so that Israel would see it as a useful ally instead of an easy enemy to overthrow. She could not afford to anger Israel, but neither could she allow Sheba to look weak in comparison. As much as she had loved hearing all of Tamrin's stories about Solomon, she was by no means a fool. Her heart might be falling for him, but her mind was still suspicious that perhaps Tamrin had been exaggerating after all. She would have to test this king carefully before she could learn from him, and she would have to be diplomatic in her dealings with him.

To achieve her goal of impressing Israel while maintaining friendly relations with the mighty nation, Makeda had a massive gift prepared for Solomon from the riches of her country: gold, precious stones, and an enormous amount of spices. It took almost 800 camels, alongside plenty of mules and donkeys, to load up all of the precious items that the queen was taking to Israel. And so, in a great train of beasts of burden—as unlike Tamrin, the queen would be traveling on land—Makeda and her vast number of attendants set forth.

She did look back once, gazing at the green jewel that was Sheba, as she prepared to head into the desert that lay between her country and Israel. For a moment, all she wanted was to run back to her safe palace and hope that her knowledge would be enough to face whatever challenges her reign had yet to bring. But something was calling her north; her heart was dragging her in the direction of this wise king who could answer all of her questions. So, she looked ahead again and kept her eyes fixed forward until the dust cloud of their passing swallowed them whole.

Chapter 6 – Encountering Solomon

Illustration II: Solomon and the Queen of Sheba by Giovanni de Min. The queen's appearance is unlikely to be ethnically correct in this illustration.

Things could hardly have gotten any better for King Solomon, yet somehow, he felt that there was something missing.

The great project to which the king had devoted years of planning and construction, the Holy Temple he'd built in Jerusalem to the God of Israel, was complete at last. Hundreds of men had worked together to produce it, and precious materials had been gathered from all around the known world in order to build it. Solomon sat on his throne, remembering the terrifying and magnificent day that the

Spirit of God had appeared to him in the Holy Temple, announcing His presence there. He knew that he'd completed what his father David had started and that his reign was already one of the most awe-inspiring in the ancient world. There were no enemies standing against Israel; King Hiram of Tyre had helped him to build the temple, and even the Pharaoh of Egypt, the ruler whose ancestors had once held the Israelites captive, had conquered the Canaanites on King Solomon's behalf and even given his own daughter in marriage to Solomon. The king himself was living in the lap of luxury. His people were prospering, and so was he, with stables full of priceless horses, treasuries piled with mountains of gold and silver, and houses filled with wives and concubines. He had everything he could possibly have wanted—except he didn't. There was something that he hadn't yet found in his wives or his wealth or his wisdom, and he didn't know yet what it was.

He thought back to the merchant that had brought some of the materials he'd used to build the temple: Tamrin, a dark-skinned, quick-witted man who had the look of a seasoned traveler and adventurer about him. He was suspicious of everyone, except there was one person that he seemed to hold in the highest regard: his queen, Makeda. Solomon wondered what made her so different that Tamrin would respect her so much. Was she perhaps a tyrant who inspired fear in her subjects? It seemed like the wonderful things that Tamrin had told him about her were far too good to be true.

Solomon didn't know. But he hoped, one day, to find out.

* * * *

When that day came, Solomon was awed.

King Solomon's throne room was beautifully decorated, as was befitting for the magnificence of the rest of his city. Its floor gleamed, constructed out of glass so finely polished that it shimmered like water. Details about the rest of the room have been lost to history, but there were likely pillars of expensive wood carved in fine detail, as well as purple draping and a gilded throne.

He watched from the windows of the splendid room as the great train of camels made its way toward his city on the hill. There were hundreds of them—he had never seen so many camels together before, not even with all his pomp and majesty. Tied one to another with goat hair ropes, the camels plodded contentedly along despite the tremendous burdens that they carried on their colorful saddles. Some of them had baby camels strapped onto their backs; Solomon knew that the mother camels were right behind those carrying the babies, and it made him think that they must have had a long journey. He sent his servants to find out who was bringing this great train of camels to his city, and when they returned, his heart flipped. It was the Queen of Sheba—the same queen who had made even Tamrin's cynical eyes light up when he spoke of her.

Solomon waited impatiently in his throne room as the train arrived. At last, he could hear the footsteps in the passage outside, and he gripped the arms of his throne in anticipation. The queen he had heard so much about was finally here.

The great doors swung open, and with attendants all around her, there she was, tall and stunning, her dark skin fascinating as it was an unusual sight for Solomon. Makeda's eyes were nervous, but her bearing was as fearless as it was proud. Her beautifully embroidered garment flowed down her slender curves, and Solomon felt awestruck as he looked at her in a way that had nothing to do with her rank and riches.

Solomon had just enough presence of mind to invite Makeda to approach the throne. She stepped forward then hesitated, spotting her reflection in the smooth glass floor. It seemed to give her pause for a moment. She gripped the front of her heavy skirt and lifted it, revealing slender ankles, and then stepped cautiously forward, toe first. She seemed startled when her foot met the cold, hard surface of the glass. Looking up at Solomon, there was a moment of awkwardness in her bearing.

The king realized that she'd first thought the glass floor was water. He hurried to reassure her, inviting her in, and she regained her composure and approached. When she reached the throne, she bowed low, her attendants all following suit. The Queen of Sheba had met King Solomon at last, and she was more than ready to test him with all of her questions. The first of which probably being what on Earth had possessed him to construct his floor out of the smoothest glass she had ever seen.

* * * *

The accounts regarding the Queen of Sheba's entrance into Jerusalem differ strongly. While both Jewish and Muslim works tell the story of the glass floor, Ethiopian manuscripts don't mention the floor at all. The Muslim account tells of demons warning Solomon that the Queen of Sheba had jinn blood in her, causing Solomon to construct the glass floor specially to trick Makeda into lifting her skirt and showing him unnaturally hairy, inhuman legs. The Bible itself does not go into detail about their first meeting, only mentioning her entrance into Jerusalem with a large gift of spices and precious metals for Solomon.

All the accounts, however, agree on one thing: Makeda's reason for visiting the venerated king. She was there to test his wisdom with her questions and decide whether she could learn from him the way Tamrin had promised. And young though she was, the queen was ready to test Solomon to his limits.

Chapter 7 – A Forbidden Union

Makeda had been in Jerusalem for several days, still resting from her journey, and even she was amazed at the sumptuousness of the quarters that Solomon had given her.

She and all her attendants had been given rooms within the royal palace itself: spacious places, beautifully decorated and elegantly furnished. That was not the end of Solomon's hospitality, however. Every day, he sent them more food than they could have ever possibly needed. Bread and oxen, fine white meal cooked in delicious gravy, wine and honey, fat poultry and mutton—even the delicacies that the king himself indulged in were sent to Makeda's quarters, accompanied by singers and entertainers. Makeda had grown up in the lap of luxury and never wanted for anything material, but this was more than even she was used to, and she found herself enjoying her rest.

Yet she hadn't come to Jerusalem to be fed and entertained. She had come to see the king. Not much time passed before Makeda asked for an audience with him, which was quickly granted.

Once again, Makeda went to meet King Solomon in the throne room. This time, however, as she walked inside, there was none of the awkwardness and nerves that she'd shown the first time. She stepped out boldly on the glass floor, and Solomon knew what was coming next: Makeda was going to test him with riddles. This ancient ritual of asking riddles had been a part of ancient cultures for centuries, and it is still evidenced in both history and mythology today. Asking riddles was considered to be an excellent test of the wisdom, intelligence, or education of another.

They exchanged pleasantries, and Makeda got straight to business. She called her attendants in, and they brought with them two vases of flowers, which they set down on the shining floor at the farthest end of the room. Her expression was openly and charmingly challenging the king to live up to his reputation as she told Solomon that one of the vases contained real flowers; the others had been skillfully made from fabric and other materials. His first riddle was to figure out which was which without rising from his throne.

Solomon didn't need to consider the question for long. He turned to his own attendants. "Open the window," he ordered.

Exchanging dubious glances, the attendants did as they were told. A warm breeze rushed through the room, running its fingers through Makeda's thick, dark hair. She watched in awe as a gentle buzzing filled the air, and one by one, bees came in from the hot sunshine, attracted by the smell of flowers. They went straight for the vase of real flowers and perched there, searching for the nectar, their delicate wings buzzing as they moved from one flower to the next.

Makeda tore her gaze away from the tiny insects to meet King Solomon's eyes. He didn't have to say anything. His smile said it all: he was ready for whatever she had to throw at him.

Through her wonder, Makeda pulled herself together. Over the buzzing of the bees, she asked her next question. "What is evil?" she asked.

Solomon's answer was instantaneous. "The eyes of the Lord in every place monitor good and evil, and in them is their definition."

Makeda paused. Tamrin had told her about this God that Solomon served. She wondered if He had anything to do with the confidence in the king's voice.

"What is the most powerful organ of the body?" she asked.

"Death and life are in the power of the tongue," said Solomon quickly with the certainty of a man whose single word could order an execution or begin a battle.

"Seven leave and nine enter," said Makeda. "Two pour out the draught, and only one drinks."

Solomon's eyes were intense, and Makeda realized that her heart was beating faster. "Seven are the days of a woman's menstruation," he said. "Nine are the months of her pregnancy. Her two breasts nourish the child, and the babe is the one that drinks."

Makeda grinned. Solomon was doing well, but she still had plenty of riddles up her sleeve for him. Yet in her heart, she knew that he'd already proven himself wise enough to teach her everything she wanted to know.

* * * *

Their visits continued on an almost daily basis. He would come to her, or she would go to him. She was always surrounded by attendants, yet every time Makeda looked at him, her heart would beat faster. She knew by the way that Solomon gazed at her that he felt the same, but she forced herself to stay focused on the task at hand. Makeda had come to learn wisdom so that she could govern Sheba wisely, not so that she could fall in love. Forcing the idea aside, she stayed attentive to what she was learning from him, and it awed her.

The precepts that the king taught her all centered on his God, and the more Makeda—a worshiper of the sun and moon, like the rest of her nation—heard from Solomon, the more she wanted to learn. He taught her lessons about humility and gentleness, showing her what it meant to govern a nation the likes of Israel the way he'd learned to do from his great father David, and also—according to the Ethiopian account—likening himself to a lowly laborer. He told Makeda that he was a man just like any other, but the more time she spent with him, the more she began to realize that he was unlike any other man she'd ever met. And judging by the stream of compliments he gave her, Solomon was just as taken with her.

Like David, Solomon had one great weakness, and also like his father, it was women. And Makeda, it would turn out, would be no different.

* * * *

Makeda had been living in the royal palace of Jerusalem for several months, and she knew that the time was coming when she would have to return to Sheba. Solomon, too, knew that the queen had to return to her country. By this point, she had learned much about ruling; she had also adopted the God of Israel as her own. According to Solomon, however, her instruction was not yet complete. He invited her into his own dining hall, ostensibly to show her the inner workings of his administration—but he also had an ulterior motive.

When Makeda came to the inner chambers, she was delighted to find that Solomon had set up a private space for her where she could see without being seen. It was as luxurious as everything else the king had done for her; there was purple draping, incense, and the heavenly scent of myrrh. She took her place there and spent all day watching as the king and his servants dined and met with other dignitaries.

It was late in the evening by the time everyone else left. Solomon approached Makeda's secret place and spoke with her. "Rest here until daybreak," he entreated her.

Makeda saw the gleam in his eyes. "Swear to me that you won't take me by force," she said. "I am a maiden—and I don't want to travel back to my people with the shame of losing my virginity in this way. Swear by your God, the God of Israel."

"I swear that I won't take you by force," Solomon agreed, "but you must swear that you won't take anything in my house."

Makeda shook her head, laughing. Why would she want to steal anything from Solomon, she asked, laughingly agreeing to his request. If she had known the plan behind what he asked, she would not have laughed.

Servants came in and readied the chamber for the two of them with Solomon's bed on one end and Makeda's on the other. But things would not stay this way for long. Craftily, Solomon had made sure that the last meal he'd served Makeda was salty and spicy, and when the queen woke in the night, she found herself with a burning thirst. She spotted a bowl of water in the chamber and sighed with relief. Getting up, she padded over to the bowl and lifted it to her lips.

That was when Solomon rose, startling the queen. His eyes flickered with delight. "Why have you broken your oath?" he demanded.

We will never know what exactly was going through Makeda's mind at that moment. Was she afraid? Did she realize what she had done with horror or with a secret joy?

Either way, the result was the same. "I've sinned against you," she told Solomon. "You are free from your oath."

And Solomon took her hand and led her to bed.

Chapter 8 – Joy on the Journey Home

Illustration II: A 17th-century artist's impression of the Queen of Sheba leaving Israel. While the Kebra Nagast has the queen travel by camel, some accounts say that she arrived in Israel by ship.

Sheba beckoned, but Makeda found herself hesitating as she stood in a hidden nook just outside the royal palace of Jerusalem. This time, her entourage for the journey home was vast. Six thousand camels stood waiting, ready to start the long trip back to Sheba, and they were so laden with everything that Makeda could have desired—precious metals, gemstones, beautifully embroidered garments—that six thousand was almost not enough. Makeda was about to bring a tremendous gift home to her people, and it was not only in the form of the material things that the camels bore. Her mind and heart were filled with the instructions that Solomon had given her, and she was excited to get back home and apply everything that she had learned.

Yet she still found herself hovering, a little reluctant to get on her camel and leave. Secreted away just outside the palace, she gazed up into Solomon's enchanting eyes, and memories of the night they'd spent together stirred in her heart.

Solomon had taken her aside for a moment, out of the loud musical ceremony with which he was seeing her off. His dark eyes gleamed as he worked the delicate ring off his little finger and held it out to her. "Take this so that you'll never forget me," he murmured, sliding it over her finger. "And if it so be that you bear a son to me, let this ring be a sign to him, and let him come to me." He paused, emotion clouding his face, knowing that he might never see the beautiful queen again. "Remember everything that I've told you, and worship God with all your heart, and perform His will."

Makeda knew that this was goodbye. She was ready to go home, but she knew that a great piece of her heart would stay behind with this bewitching king.

"May God be with you," said Solomon roughly. "Go in peace."

So, Makeda walked away from him, the only man she'd ever loved. She got on her camel and turned back to Sheba, and as the camel walked away, she felt the stirrings of a new life deep inside her.

* * * *

The long journey back to Sheba grew more and more arduous for the pregnant queen. With the thousands of camels to manage, there always seemed to be something slowing them down, and Makeda grew more and more anxious as her belly swelled with every passing day. She was not going to be able to give birth to her child in Sheba. Instead, to her horror, she realized that she was going to bring her firstborn forth somewhere along the way.

The pains of labor seized her nine months and five days after she'd left the safety of Jerusalem. Attended by a nurse—not the medical professional that the nurses of today are, but a woman who was ready to nurse Makeda's child on her behalf—the young queen was forced to birth her baby somewhere along the road, although she would possibly have been able to stop in a city. Still, she would have been surrounded by strangers with no family and possibly no friends nearby; apart from the baby that was making its entrance into the world, Makeda had no family. She would only have this child, and she had to birth it alone, with no medications and no help.

Makeda knew that she would likely never journey back to Jerusalem again. She also knew that there would never be another man for her, not after Solomon. The future of her entire kingdom hinged upon the birth of this child, and when, finally, the nurse placed the baby into Makeda's arms, she could only rejoice as she laid eyes on the healthy little baby. What was more, it was a little boy. Sheba now had a male heir.

The baby's name depends on the account you read; in Muslim accounts, he was known as Ibn al-Hakim, or the "Son of the Wise," while in the *Kebra Nagast*, he was Bayna-Lehkem. In history, however, he is most popularly known by his simplest name: Menelik, later Menelik I.

With the baby being safely cared for by the nurse, Makeda journeyed home to a country that welcomed her and her infant son with open arms. Menelik was illegitimate under Jewish law, but the people of Sheba had little regard for such things; a son was a son, and they welcomed him home as their crown prince. They were delighted to see their queen again and were especially excited to see the gifts she brought home. Wealthy and prosperous Sheba was not only even wealthier and more prosperous now—its queen was home, and the whole country rejoiced.

* * * *

Twelve-year-old Menelik had grown up surrounded by nothing but the best. His mother made sure that he had everything his heart desired—and several things that his heart certainly didn't. Chief among these was an education. Menelik would far rather have been out riding and hunting than stuck in the opulent rooms of the palace, listening to his tutors drone on and on about subjects that bored him. But he dutifully attended his lessons because his mother told him that he would be king one day.

The only good thing about lessons, from Menelik's point of view, was his friends. He had grown up among a group of noble boys his age, and they played, fought, and fooled around together. One thing he always noticed was how the other boys all had fathers. Some of their fathers had died in battles or accidents, but even those boys spoke of them often, and Menelik couldn't understand why he didn't have a father. He eventually began to ask, and his shy curiosity led him to ask his friends before anyone else.

"Who is my father?" he asked them one day as they were walking through the palace, the other boys pushing and jostling as they teased each other.

"Solomon the King," one of the boys answered him.

Menelik's father was a king? He had to find out more. He hurried back to his mother and asked her about it at the first opportunity.

Makeda was dismayed when Menelik asked her who his father was. She turned the ring that Solomon had given her around and around on her finger, knowing that Menelik's curiosity about his father might lead him all the way to Israel, and she knew from experience how long that journey was.

She stared at the boy. It had been almost thirteen long years since she'd turned away from the palace at Jerusalem and the man who'd captured her heart, and with every day that passed, Menelik looked more and more like his father. He had those same eyes, intense and serious, and even all these years later, Makeda felt an agonizing pang of longing for the king she'd loved. She couldn't let Menelik go. He was all that she had left of Solomon and of her own family. "I am your father and your mother," she said angrily, trying to scare him into dropping the subject.

But Menelik didn't let it go. He continued to pester and pester his mother until she finally told him. "His country is far away, and the road there is very difficult; wouldn't you rather stay here?" she asked.

Possibly seeing how his questioning had grieved his mother, Menelik let it go.

But not for long.

Chapter 9 – A New King

Makeda knew the moment that Menelik walked in that she couldn't put it off any longer. Her boy was going to Israel, and there was little that she could do to stop him.

She gazed at him with sorrow, remembering the day—ten years ago now—that he'd first asked her about his father. She'd been just as terrified to lose him then as she was now, but now he wasn't a boy anymore but a strong young man. He had his father's broad shoulders and pure voice; the flash of his eyes held the same intelligence, and Makeda knew that he'd grown into a worthy young prince. Yet the prince's heart longed to know more about where he had come from. He had grown up hearing the stories about his mother's family, but his father was a stranger to him except for the awed whispers of everyone who knew the story of Solomon's wisdom and how he had imparted it to Queen Makeda. His questioning heart wouldn't rest until he'd seen his father's face.

Menelik saw his mother's sorrow in her eyes. He spoke to her gently. "I will go and look upon the face of my father," he told her, "and I will come back here by the will of God, the Lord of Israel."

Makeda smiled. He sounded so much like Solomon when he talked about God; she had raised him according to Solomon's teachings, after all. She called for Tamrin, and he limped into the room. Even more grizzled now than he had been a quarter of a century earlier when he made his first trip to Israel, Tamrin was still faithfully serving the queen as the chief of her merchants. "Get ready for your journey," she told him. "And take this young man with you, because he won't stop asking me to go. Take him to the King and bring him back here in safety, if God wills it."

* * * *

King Solomon stood in his royal palace gazing out of the window at the great city of Jerusalem. The mighty Holy Temple, completed years ago, towered above the other buildings in its splendor and grandeur; within, Solomon had seen the presence of God and had hidden a thousand holy treasures, including the Ark of the Covenant. The holiest of all holy objects, the Ark contained numerous holy items, including the tablets on which the Ten Commandments had been written. It was hidden deep within the temple in an inner chamber where only the high priest ever entered, which was only on the rarest of occasions.

The Ark was not the only treasure that Solomon had gathered in Jerusalem. His stables were filled with the best and proudest Egyptian horses; his houses overflowed with women, as he was now married to 700 wives and had 300 concubines. Although he had had little luck with children, at least he did have a seven-year-old heir, little Rehoboam. His treasuries were filled with the most elaborate riches, and his coffers were spilling over with gold. Even his mind and heart were filled with the most precious and priceless thing of all: wisdom. Yet there was one thing that the richest king on Earth wanted, one beautiful treasure that he had been missing for decades, and her name was Makeda. He wondered where she was now, if she had even made it safely home to Sheba. If she remembered him the way that he remembered her.

There was a commotion outside, and King Solomon turned around to find a few wide-eyed palace guards hurrying into the room. Spies had come to the palace from the province of Gaza, they said, and they had a very perplexing reason for riding to Jerusalem: they were coming to see if King Solomon was in his palace because, according to some of the people of Gaza, the king was in Gaza.

Infuriated, Solomon ordered the spies to be brought to him and explain themselves. There must be an impostor in Gaza, and who knows what trouble such an individual was going to cause.

The spies were brought before Solomon, and he demanded to know their story. Trembling, one of the spies threw himself on the ground in front of the king. "Hail, may the royal father live!" he exclaimed nervously. "Our country is disturbed, because a merchant has come to it that looks exactly like you in every way, without the smallest alteration or variation."

Solomon listened to the spy describing this merchant, and hope leaped in his heart. The similarity that the spy talked about was such that Solomon knew that there was only one reasonable explanation: The man had to be his son. His son by the Queen of Sheba, the woman that Solomon's heart had always longed for.

* * * *

Solomon sent the commander of his army, Benaiah, to Gaza with all haste, ordering him to bring the young man to the palace as quickly as possible. Menelik found himself being ushered to Jerusalem as fast as Benaiah could bring him; Solomon was desperate to see him, and when he finally laid eyes on his firstborn, he was awed and delighted. The entire court was struck speechless by the resemblance between father and son.

Immediately, Solomon decided to make it his business to hold on to Menelik for all he was worth. He had let the Queen of Sheba herself slip through his fingers, but he wasn't about to let the same thing happen with his oldest child. Bestowing countless gifts on Menelik, including gorgeous garments embroidered with gold, Solomon practically begged him to stay. He wanted to make Menelik the King of Israel, and for a young man whose future lay wide open before him, it must have been a tempting proposition.

But back home in Sheba, there was an aging queen pining for her boy, the only family she had left. And Menelik remembered his promise to his mother. Despite Solomon's continued entreaties, Menelik held firm: he was going home to Sheba, just as he'd promised. He had not come to Israel in order to be made its king. He had come to meet his father, and he had one request to ask of him: that he would be crowned as the King of Sheba using Israelite rituals and ceremonies. The request was not entirely Menelik's; instead, Queen Makeda herself had asked for this to be done so that Sheba would be ruled by a king who had been consecrated and made holy, just like the King of Israel whom she loved so fiercely.

King Menelik I left Jerusalem to an outpouring of dismay. Solomon had done as Makeda had asked and crowned Menelik the King of Sheba with tremendous pomp and ceremony; the high priest in the temple himself had given Menelik instructions for his rule. What was more, Solomon sent Menelik home with the firstborns of all his nobles in order for them to rule in Sheba just as their families ruled in Israel. It was a great procession that left for Sheba, and while Menelik and his friends rejoiced, all of Jerusalem wept and howled at the loss of the young man who could have been King of Israel. According to some accounts, it was not just himself and the other young people that Menelik took back to Sheba. The Ark of the Covenant itself was included in the list of treasures that Menelik had in his procession, smuggled out of the temple by some of Menelik's retinue. The *Kebra Nagast* tells how an angel told them to steal the Ark and carry it off to Sheba, and to this day, Ethiopia claims to have the Ark hidden in a tiny chapel in the village of Aksum, guarded by devoted monks who are never allowed to set foot outside the chapel until the day they die.

So, Menelik returned to Sheba and to a great rejoicing. Sheba had gained not only a newly anointed king but also a vast array of young nobles who had grown up at the feet of Solomon's wisdom. Makeda was overjoyed to have her son back. She surrendered her throne to him, and a son of Solomon sat down upon the throne of Sheba, of Ethiopia. There was great rejoicing, and the whole palace was filled with a joyous celebration.

As for Makeda herself, the beautiful, wise, and courageous Queen of Sheba, her story faded into obscurity once her son took the throne. She had gone to Jerusalem for wisdom to protect her country, and now, she had proven that she had done even better than that: She had brought home an heir educated like one of Israel's greatest kings, an heir whose coronation promised peace and safety for Sheba in the generations to come. Makeda had fulfilled her mission to protect her people.

Wisdom was not all that she had found in Israel, though. She watched the celebration and gazed at her son upon the throne. He was in every way the image of his father, and when she closed her eyes, she could still see the gleam in Solomon's dark eyes that night. A night that she would never forget.

Conclusion

Almost nothing is known of Makeda's life after the coronation of Menelik. We can only guess that her devoted son ensured that she lived out her days in peace and safety in the country that she'd done everything to protect; yet perhaps a part of her longed forever for the man she'd left behind in Jerusalem decades ago.

The story of the Queen of Sheba is an incomplete one. We only have an educated guess at where Sheba was even located; historians doubt whether the queen herself ever existed. Accounts differ wildly on all but one thing—she came to King Solomon for wisdom, even though her own country was filled with riches, and she was tremendously impressed.

Ethiopian tradition, however, is utterly assured of the fact that her son with King Solomon was not only a king of Ethiopia—he was also the progenitor of a dynasty that, according to tradition, lasted nearly 3,000 years. Sheba became Aksum whose rulers' obscure origins makes it possible that they were, in fact, descendants of Menelik. In the Middle Ages, the Zagwe dynasty briefly took over ruling Aksum after murdering the entire royal family, apart from a single baby that was smuggled out of danger by supporters. The Zagwe dynasty was overthrown in 1270 by Yekuno Amlak, who claimed to be a descendant of Menelik, and with his rule, the official Solomonic Dynasty began.

Solomonic emperors would rule over Aksum, which became known as Ethiopia, for centuries. In fact, it was only during the Second World War that Ethiopia was invaded and occupied for the first time since the time of the Zagwes; Mussolini's Italian troops occupied the country only briefly, and the emperor, Haile Selassie, was sent into exile. Selassie was the last of the Solomonic emperors. He was deposed in 1974 and died in prison a year later.

Solomon's descendants no longer sit on the Ethiopian throne; democracy was instituted after Selassie's deposition, allowing presidents to be elected and to govern the country in a fairer and more modern manner. Yet there still remains something intensely poetic about the current president, something that connects the ancient rule of the Queen of Sheba with the Ethiopia of today. Like the fabled queen, Sahle-Work Zewde is a striking African woman proudly ruling over a magnificent country. She is the only female head of state on the entire continent.

The Queen of Sheba remains a historical figure so wreathed in mystery that she is little more than a legend. Yet her tale of courageous rule, in a time when women were denied power, and of her selfless protection of her people has a powerful quality that still makes her an inspiration thousands of years later. We might never know the real story behind the Queen of Sheba. But the story we do have—a story of a brave queen who would do anything for her people—promises to continue to ring down through the generations to come.

Here's another book by Captivating History that you might be interested in

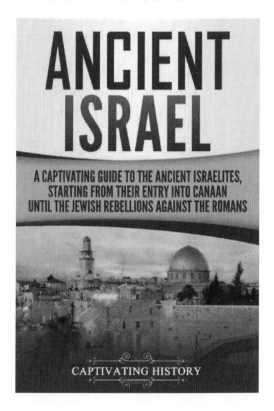

References

[1] The so-called Deuteronomists were high officials of Jerusalem—the scribes and the priests of the temple—whose job was to keep the archives, deal with diplomatic correspondence, draft laws, and make the annals. Traditionally, they are seen as the authors of the historic books in the Bible (Deuteronomist history).

[1] According to the Book of Genesis, Jacob was the patriarch of the Israelites. His name was changed to Israel ("to rule, contend, have power, prevail over") after his wrestling with an angel (Genesis 32:22–32)

[1] The land of Israel, often referred to as the Promised Land, has historically also been known as Canaan, Phoenicia, and, much later, Palestine.

[1] Jacob's twelve sons were the patriarchs of the twelve tribes of Israel.

[1] 1 Sam. 4

[1] The Canaanites were the people who inhabited ancient Israel (Canaan) before the Israelites came from their captivity in Egypt in 12 century BCE.

[1] 1 Sam. 5-7; The King James's Bible mentions "hemorrhoids," most other versions mention "tumors" instead

[1] 1 Sam. 8

[1] 1 Sam. 9:2

[1] 1 Sam. 15

[1] https://en.wikipedia.org/wiki/Tel_Dan_Stele

[1] 1 Sam. 16

[1] 1 Sam. 17

[1] The famous statue by Michelangelo, unveiled in 1504 in Florence, depicting the biblical hero; image source: Wikimedia Commons https://commons.wikimedia.org/wiki/File:David_09.jpg

[1] http://articles.latimes.com/2013/oct/31/opinion/la-oe-badenmoss-gladwell-goliath-20131031

[1] 1 Sam. 24

[1] 1 Sam. 25

[1] 2 Sam. 1

[1] Exodus 7; Rockwood, Camilla, ed. (2007). "Aaron." Chambers Biographical Dictionary (8th ed.). Edinburgh, UK: Chambers Harrap Publishers Ltc.

[1] 2 Sam. 5

[1] 2 Sam. 6

[1] 2 Sam.

[1] 2 Sam. 11

[1] As above

[1] 2 Sam. 13

[1] 2 Sam. 14

[1] 2 Sam. 15

[1] 2 Sam. 18

[1] 2 Sam. 16

[1] 2 Sam. 18

[1] 2 Sam. 24

[1] 1 Kings 1

[1] As above

[1] 1 Kings 2

[1] As above

[1] 1 Kings 3

[1] As above

[1] As above

[1] Wikimedia Commons https://en.wikipedia.org/wiki/File:Salomons_dom.jpg

[1] 1 Kings 9

[1] 1 Kings 5

[1] As above

[1] 1 Kings 11

[1] 1 Kings 12

[1] As above; see chapter 1

[1] 1 Kings 14; 2 Chron. 12

[1] http://www.reshafim.org.il/ad/egypt/sheshonqi.htm

[1] Stuart Munro-Hay, The Quest for the Ark of the Covenant, Tauris, 2005

[1] David Van Biema, A Lead on the Ark of the Covenant, Time.com, 2008

[1] Inscriptions such as the Nimrud Tablet contain detailed account of Assyrian and Babylonian king's invasions.

[1] https://en.wikipedia.org/wiki/Mesha_Stele

[1] 1 Kings 16

[1] 1 Kings 18 and 19

[1] 2 Kings 2

[1] 2 Kings 8

[1] 2 Kings 9

[1] 2 Kings 10

[1] 2 Kings 11

[1] 2 Kings 13

[1] 2 Kings 15

[1] Num. 21

[1] 2 Kings 15

[1] 2 Kings 21

[1] 2 Kings 22-23

[1] 2 Chron. 35

[1] 2 Kings

A History of Israel in the Old Testament Period. Jagersma, Henk. Trans. John Bowden. Philadelphia: Fortress Press, 1983.

An Introduction to the Old Testament. Harrison, R.K. Grand Rapids, MI: Eerdmans. 1969.

Eerdmans Dictionary of the Bible. Freedman, David Noel, ed. Grand Rapids, MI: W. B. Eerdmans Publishing Company, 2000.

Reading the Old Testament: An Introduction; Second Edition. Lawrence Boadt, Richard Clifford and Daniel Harrington. Paulist Press, 2012.

The Oxford Bible Commentary. Barton, John and John Muddiman, eds. New York: Oxford University Press, 2001.

The Wiley Blackwell Companion to Ancient Israel. Susan Niditch (editor). Malden, MA: Wiley Blackwell, 2016.

The Holy Bible, King James Version (https://www.biblegateway.com/)

Kebra Nagast, as translated by Sir E. A. Wallis Budge (http://www.yorku.ca/inpar/kebra_budge.pdf)

http://jhodgesagame.blogspot.com/2013/07/the-queen-of-sheba-kingdom-of-dmt-and.html

https://www.britannica.com/place/Ethiopia/Sports-and-recreation#ref419469

https://theancientweb.com/explore/africa/ethopia/

https://www.ancient.eu/Kingdom_of_Saba/

https://www.africa.com/great-ancient-african-queens/

http://freemasonry.bcy.ca/texts/gmd1999/sheba.html

https://www.pbs.org/mythsandheroes/myths_four_sheba.html

http://www.womeninthebible.net/women-bible-old-new-testaments/queen-of-sheba/

http://www.blackhistoryinthebible.com/blurred-lines/king-menelik-i-the-solomonic-dynasty-and-the-ark-of-the-covenant/

https://www.geni.com/people/Menelik-I-da-Ethiopia/6000000002518586281

https://www.japantimes.co.jp/life/2013/06/30/travel/how-the-ark-of-the-covenant-got-to-ethiopia/#.XOzftLPv7ak

https://www.theguardian.com/lifeandstyle/2010/oct/09/haile-selassie-ethiopia-king-solomon

https://www.britannica.com/topic/Solomonid-dynasty

https://ethiopianhistory.com/Solomonic_Dynasty/

https://www.nytimes.com/1986/02/04/science/was-there-a-queen-of-sheba-evidence-makes-her-more-likely.html

https://www.aljazeera.com/news/2018/10/sahle-work-zewde-ethiopia-female-president-181027134726828.html

Illustration I: The Queen of Sheba from a manuscript (Staats- und Universitätsbibliothek Göttingen, 2 Cod. Ms. Philos. 63, Cim., fol. 122r) of Bellifortis by Conrad Kyeser.
https://commons.wikimedia.org/wiki/File:Bellifortis_Queen_of_Sheba.jpg

Illustration II: By Giovanni Demin (1789-1859) -
http://www.artrenewal.org/pages/artwork.php?artworkid=10389, Public Domain,
https://commons.wikimedia.org/w/index.php?curid=3520809

Illustration III: By Claude Lorrain (1605-1682)
https://en.wikipedia.org/wiki/File:Claude_Lorrain_008.jpg

https://www.biblegateway.com

https://www.history.com/topics/religion/history-of-christianity

https://en.wikipedia.org/wiki/History_of_Christianity

https://www.bible-history.com

https://edition.cnn.com/2013/11/12/world/christianity-fast-facts/index.html

https://www.vaticannews.va/en/pope/news/2019-04/homily-of-fr-cantalamessa-for-good-friday-full-text.html

https://www.bible.com/bible/compare/ISA.9.6-7

http://www.archpitt.org/the-immaculate-conception-the-conception-of-st-anne-when-she-conceived-the-holy-mother-of-god-according-to-the-ruthenian-tradition/

https://www.youtube.com/watch?v=yL-8lRHlEXc

http://www.quranicstudies.com/historical-jesus/the-virginal-conception-of-jesus/

https://www.biography.com/religious-figure/saint-mark

https://www.cbsnews.com/news/the-unexpected-pagan-origins-of-popular-christmas-traditions/

http://evidenceforchristianity.org/

https://www.catholic.org

https://www.whychristmas.com

https://biblearchaeologyreport.com/2018/08/09/did-first-century-nazareth-exist/

https://www.christianitytoday.com/history/2018/december/putting-christ-back-in-christmas-not-enough-nativity-americ.html

https://www.levitt.com/essays/language

https://www.ucg.org/the-good-news/good-news-interview-carsten-peter-thiede-when-was-the-new-testament-written

https://www.franciscanmedia.org/john-the-baptist-distinct-gospel-portraits/

http://www.bbc.co.uk/religion/religions/christianity/holydays/christmas_1.shtml

http://www.ncregister.com

www.biblicalarchaeology.org

https://thirdmill.org

www.baslibrary.org

https://catholicexchange.com

www.smithsonianmag.com

https://www.smithsonianmag.com/history/who-was-mary-magdalene-119565482/

https://www.ancient.eu

https://kids.britannica.com

https://www.historytoday.com/archive/crusades/fourth-crusade-and-sack-constantinople

https://medievalchurch.org.uk/pdf/e-books/maclear/christian-missions-middles-ages_maclear.pdf

www.medievalchronicles.com

www.pewresearch.org

https://www.ancient.eu/Saladin/

www.pewforum.org

https://www.intellectualtakeout.org/article/5-causes-protestant-reformation-besides-indulgences

http://www.evidenceunseen.com/theology/ecclesiology/understanding-american-protestant-denominations/

https://www.christianpost.com/news/the-15-largest-protestant-denominations-in-the-united-states.html

https://sites.dartmouth.edu/ancientbooks/2016/05/24/medieval-book-production-and-monastic-life/

i *The Encyclopedia Britannica.* University Press, Cambridge, England.

ii This term derives from the fact that the educated families and scribes in charge of transcribing the ancient Tanakh texts were called *Masoretics*.

iii http://www.papalencyclicals.net/pius09/p9ineff.htm

iv https://www.psephizo.com/biblical-studies/when-was-jesus-born/

v https://www.psephizo.com/biblical-studies/when-was-jesus-born/

vi https://www.desiringgod.org/interviews/truth-or-fiction-did-herod-really-slaughter-baby-boys-in-bethlehem

vii https://www.britannica.com/biography/Jesus

viii https://www.smithsonianmag.com/history/who-was-mary-magdalene-119565482/

ix https://vatican.com/The-Holy-Spear/

x https://www.catholic.com/qa/why-did-god-change-sauls-name-to-paul

xi Maclear, George Frederick, M.A. A *History of Christian Missions During the Middle Ages.* MacMillan and Co., Cambridge and London, 1863.

xii Saladin's complete name was Ṣalāḥ al-Dīn Yūsuf ibn Ayyūb ("Righteousness of the Faith, Joseph, Son of Job"), also called al-Malik al-Nāṣir Ṣalāḥ al-Dīn Yūsuf I.

xiii Manchester, William. *A World Lit Only by Fire.* Little, Brown and Co., 1992.

xiv Watson, Peter. *Ideas: A History from Fire to Freud,* 2005.

xv https://www.smithsonianmag.com/history/americas-true-history-of-religious-tolerance-61312684/

xvi Pew Research Center's Forum on Religion & Public Life. GLOBAL CHRISTIANITY: A REPORT ON THE SIZE AND DISTRIBUTION OF THE WORLD'S CHRISTIAN POPULATION, 2011.

xvii https://www.pewforum.org/2011/12/19/global-christianity-exec/#_ftn1

xviii https://www.pewforum.org/2010/04/15/executive-summary-islam-and-christianity-in-sub-saharan-africa/

xix The so-called Deuteronomists were high officials of Jerusalem—the scribes and the priests of the temple—whose job was to keep the archives, deal with diplomatic correspondence, draft laws, and make the annals. Traditionally, they are seen as the authors of the historic books in the Bible (Deuteronomist history).

xx According to the Book of Genesis, Jacob was the patriarch of the Israelites. His name was changed to Israel ("to rule, contend, have power, prevail over") after his wrestling with an angel (Genesis 32:22–32)

xxi The land of Israel, often referred to as the Promised Land, has historically also been known as Canaan, Phoenicia, and, much later, Palestine.

xxii Jacob's twelve sons were the patriarchs of the twelve tribes of Israel.

xxiii 1 Sam. 4

xxiv The Canaanites were the people who inhabited ancient Israel (Canaan) before the Israelites came from their captivity in Egypt in 12 century BCE.

xxv 1 Sam. 5-7; The King James's Bible mentions "hemorrhoids," most other versions mention "tumors" instead

xxvi 1 Sam. 8

xxvii 1 Sam. 9:2

xxviii 1 Sam. 15

xxix https://en.wikipedia.org/wiki/Tel_Dan_Stele

xxx 1 Sam. 16

xxxi 1 Sam. 17

xxxii The famous statue by Michelangelo, unveiled in 1504 in Florence, depicting the biblical hero; image source: Wikimedia Commons https://commons.wikimedia.org/wiki/File:David_09.jpg

xxxiii http://articles.latimes.com/2013/oct/31/opinion/la-oe-badenmoss-gladwell-goliath-20131031

xxxiv 1 Sam. 24

xxxv 1 Sam. 25

xxxvi 2 Sam. 1

xxxvii Exodus 7; Rockwood, Camilla, ed. (2007). "Aaron." Chambers Biographical Dictionary (8th ed.). Edinburgh, UK: Chambers Harrap Publishers Ltc.

xxxviii 2 Sam. 5

xxxix 2 Sam. 6

xl 2 Sam.

xli 2 Sam. 11

xlii As above

xliii 2 Sam. 13

xliv 2 Sam. 14

xlv 2 Sam. 15

xlvi 2 Sam. 18

xlvii 2 Sam. 16

xlviii 2 Sam. 18

xlix 2 Sam. 24

l 1 Kings 1

li As above

lii 1 Kings 2

liii As above

liv 1 Kings 3

lv As above

lvi As above

lvii Wikimedia Commons https://en.wikipedia.org/wiki/File:Salomons_dom.jpg

lviii 1 Kings 9

lix 1 Kings 5

[lx] As above

[lxi] 1 Kings 11

[lxii] 1 Kings 12

[lxiii] As above; see chapter 1

[lxiv] 1 Kings 14; 2 Chron. 12

[lxv] http://www.reshafim.org.il/ad/egypt/sheshonqi.htm

[lxvi] Stuart Munro-Hay, The Quest for the Ark of the Covenant, Tauris, 2005

[lxvii] David Van Biema, A Lead on the Ark of the Covenant, Time.com, 2008

[lxviii] Inscriptions such as the Nimrud Tablet contain detailed account of Assyrian and Babylonian king's invasions.

[lxix] https://en.wikipedia.org/wiki/Mesha_Stele

[lxx] 1 Kings 16

[lxxi] 1 Kings 18 and 19

[lxxii] 2 Kings 2

[lxxiii] 2 Kings 8

[lxxiv] 2 Kings 9

[lxxv] 2 Kings 10

[lxxvi] 2 Kings 11

[lxxvii] 2 Kings 13

[lxxviii] 2 Kings 15

[lxxix] Num. 21

[lxxx] 2 Kings 15

[lxxxi] 2 Kings 21

[lxxxii] 2 Kings 22-23

[lxxxiii] 2 Chron. 35

Made in the
USA
Monee, IL